# SIN

THE ART OF TRANSGRESSION

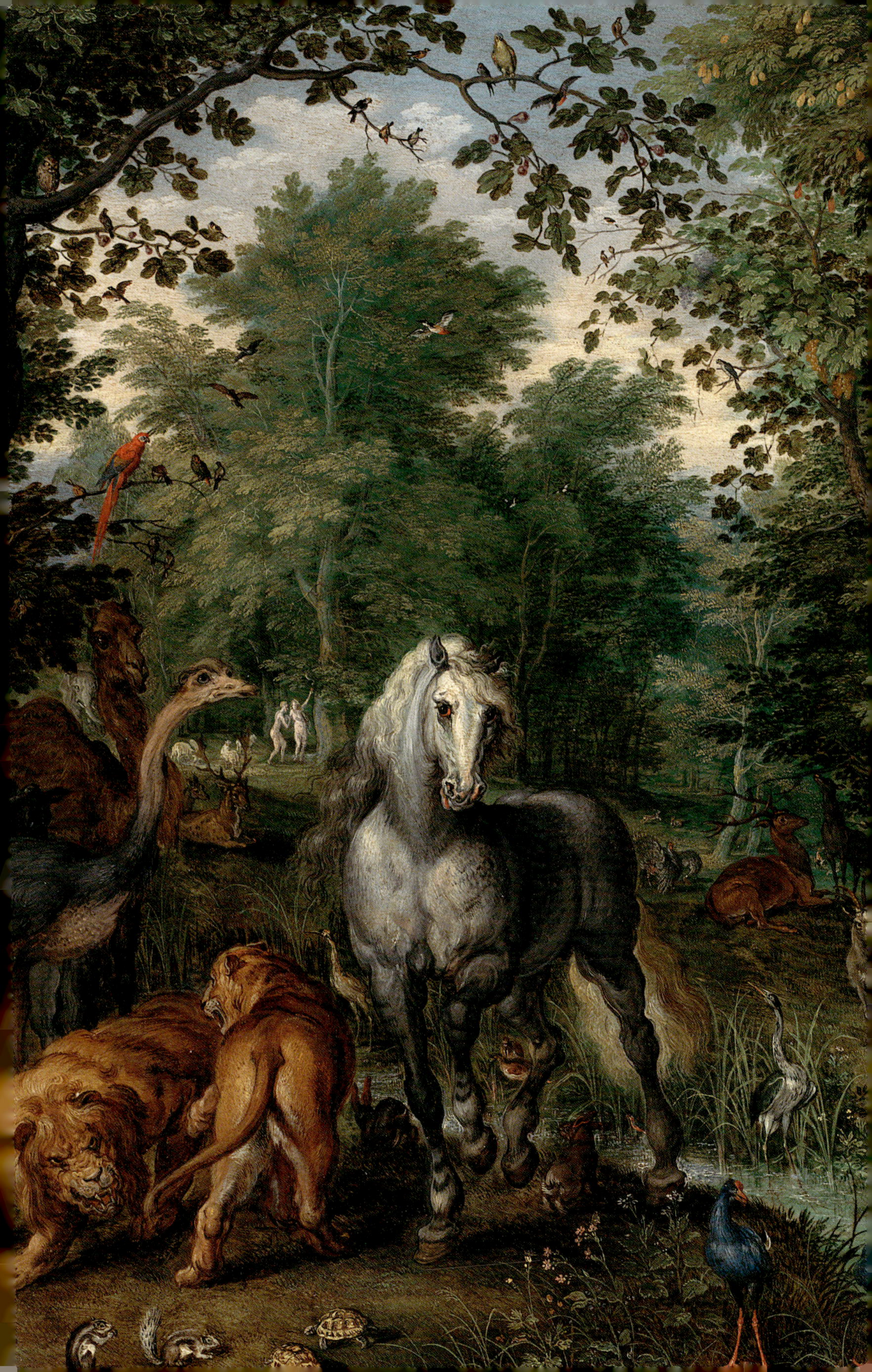

# SIN

## THE ART OF TRANSGRESSION

JOOST JOUSTRA

NATIONAL GALLERY COMPANY, LONDON
DISTRIBUTED BY YALE UNIVERSITY PRESS

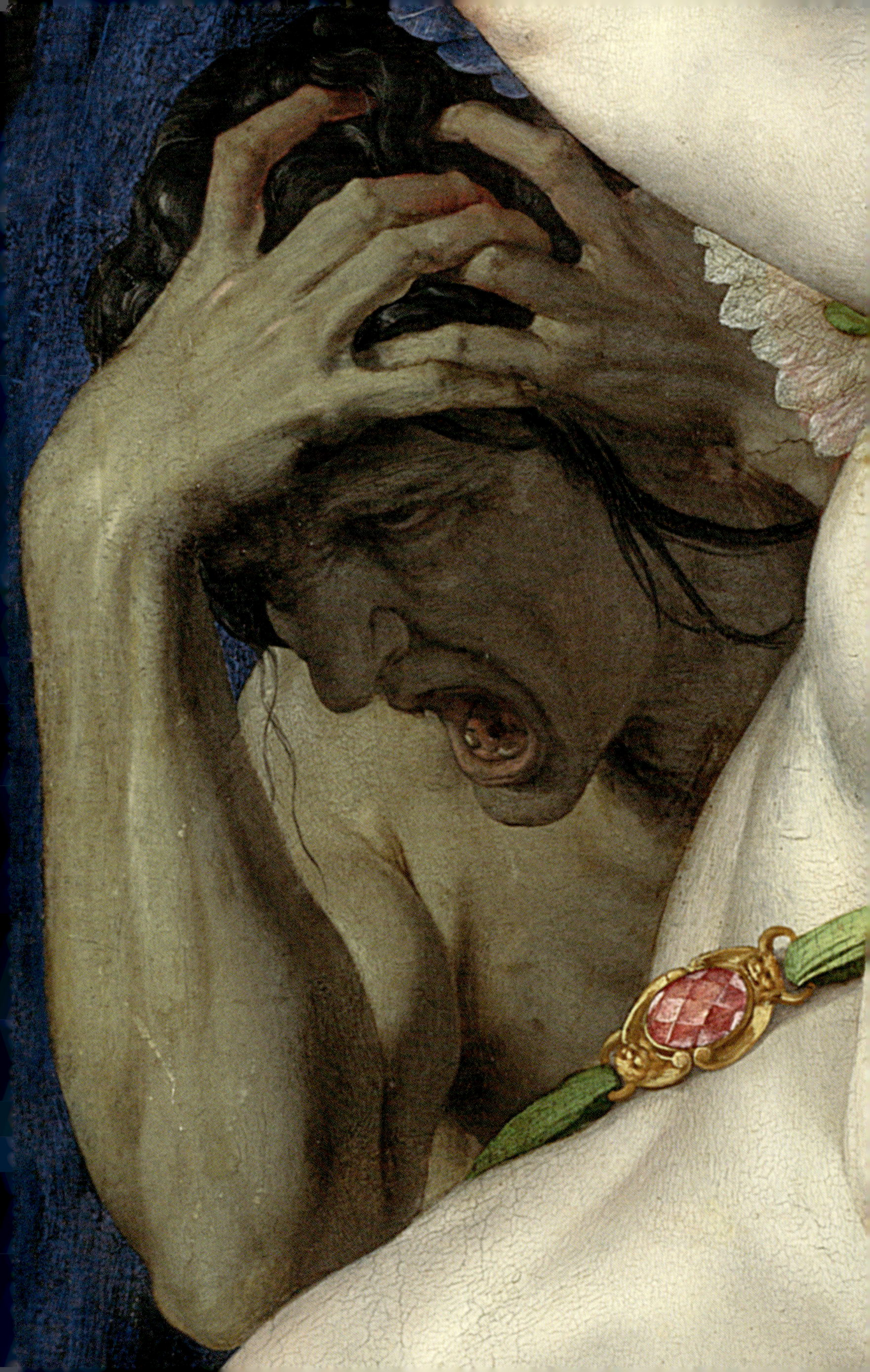

# CONTENTS

DIRECTOR'S FOREWORD 6

## SIN: THE ART OF TRANSGRESSION

**EVERYONE IS A SINNER** 9
**IN THE BEGINNING** 13
**EVE/VENUS: AN INTRODUCTION TO AMBIGUITY** 26
**THE ART OF TRANSGRESSION** 30
**THE REDEEMER** 56
**PAINTING AND REPENTING** 70
**THE FIRST TO THROW A STONE** 87

NOTES 95
BIBLIOGRAPHY 98
LIST OF EXHIBITED WORKS 102
LENDERS 102
ACKNOWLEDGEMENTS 103
PHOTOGRAPHIC CREDITS 103

# DIRECTOR'S FOREWORD

It may be surprising for visitors to the exhibition and readers of this book to see how many National Gallery pictures are bound up with the subject of sin. But it shouldn't be. Whether sin is defined as a transgression against a divine or moral law, a regrettable fault, an offence or a failure to do what is right, all of us are implicated in one way or another. Over the centuries artists have found powerful and compelling means to treat this all-enveloping condition. Lucas Cranach the Elder's Adam and Eve eating the forbidden fruit takes us back to the origins of the story, often referred to as the Fall, while Jan Steen and William Hogarth reflect with bitter-sweet irony on the consequences of excess. Pieter Bruegel the Elder focuses on Christ's forgiveness of sin and the admonition not to cast the first stone. Redemption, declares Andy Warhol, is open to all who repent, and Tracey Emin and Ron Mueck offer an ambivalent and a meditative take on this age-old theme.

I would like to thank Joost Joustra, the Howard and Roberta Ahmanson Fellow in Art and Religion at the National Gallery, for conceiving the exhibition – which, though small packs a big punch – and for writing this book. Howard and Roberta have supported numerous research and exhibition projects at the Gallery for nearly 20 years and we are very grateful to them for their ongoing friendship.

Finally, I would like to extend our gratitude to the lenders to the exhibition: The Courtauld Gallery, Manchester Art Gallery, Tracey Emin (via White Cube), Ron Mueck, Ed Freedman, and a private collection in Hong Kong.

Gabriele Finaldi
*Director*

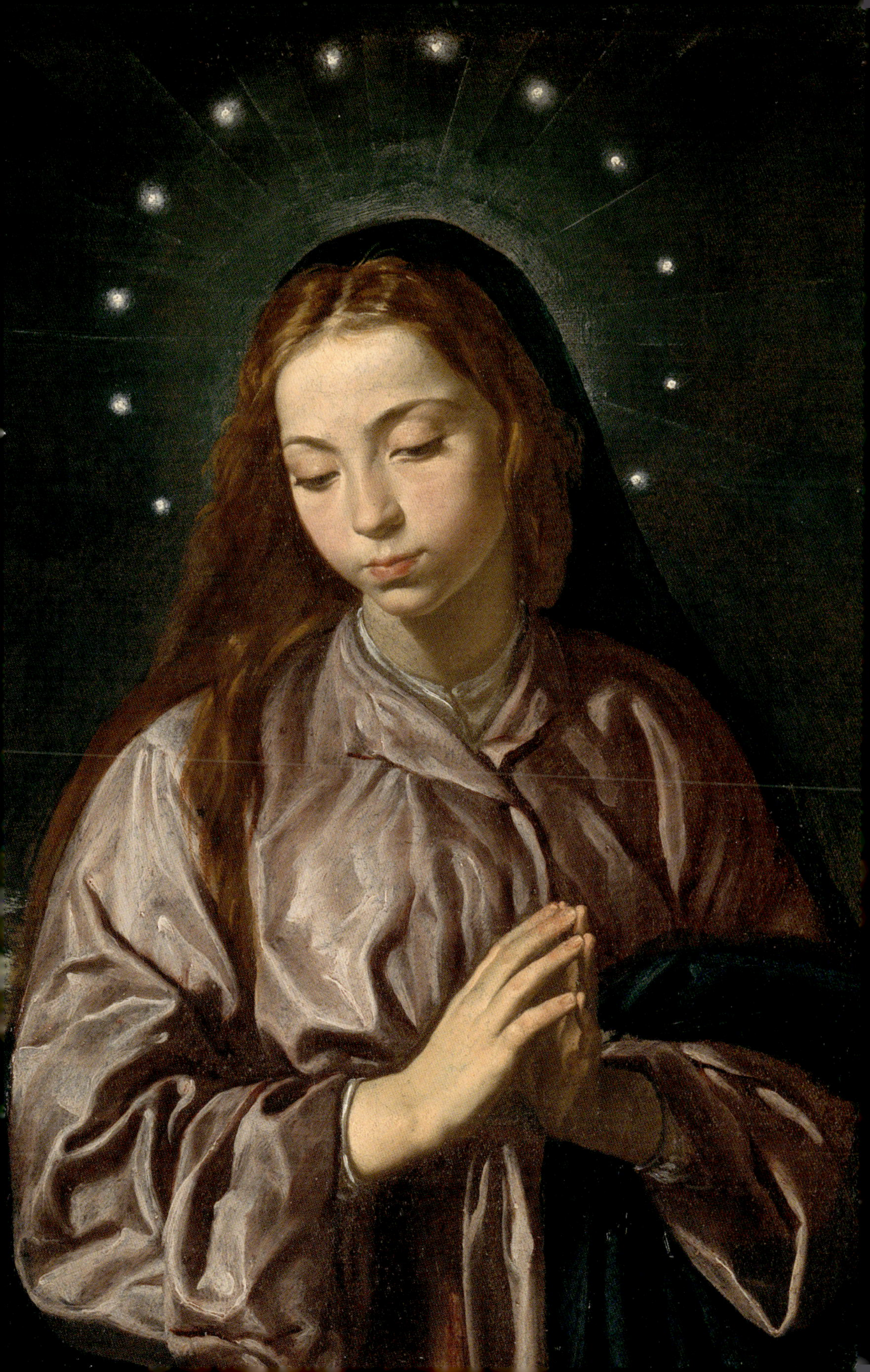

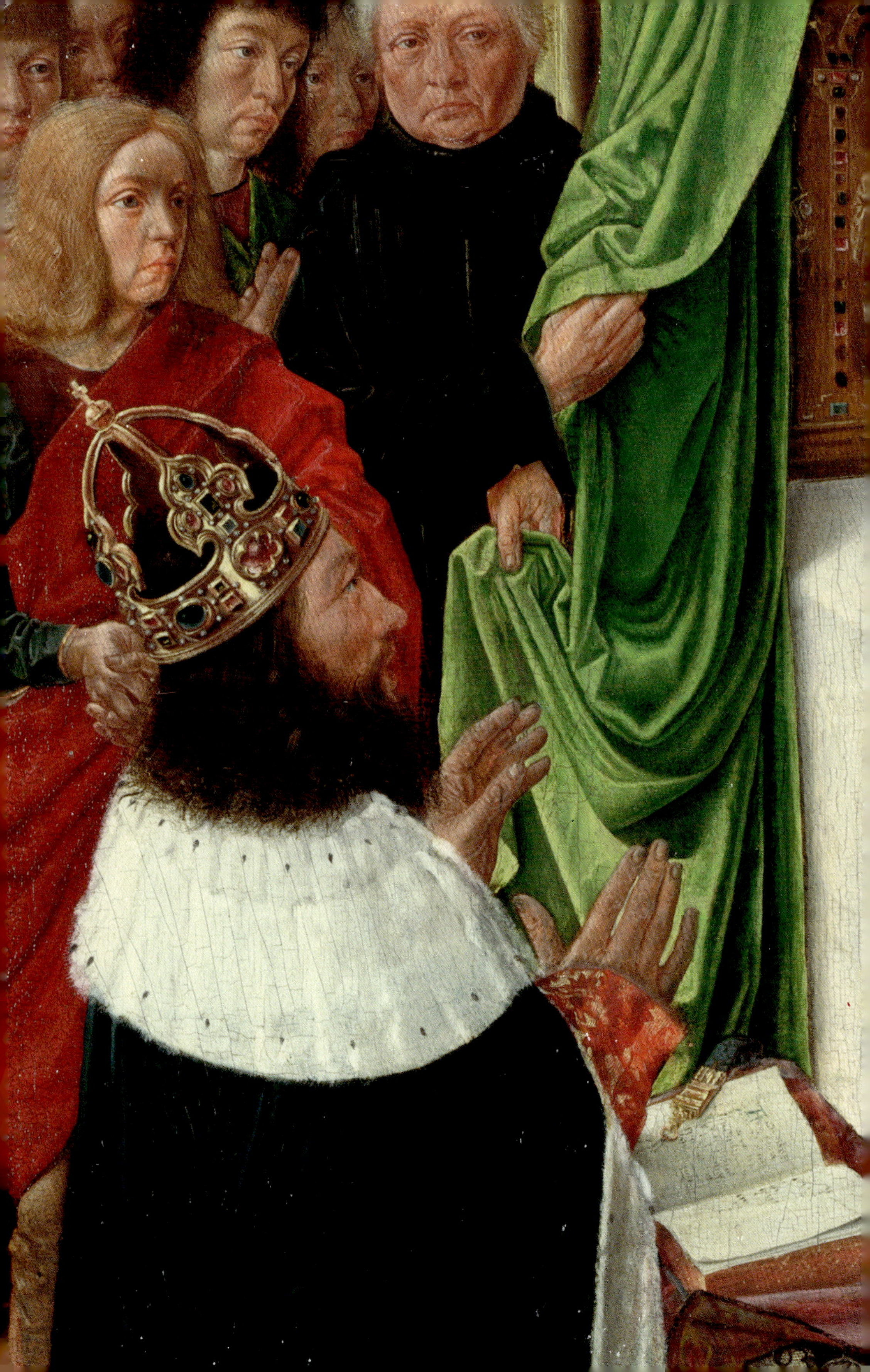

# SIN:
# THE ART OF TRANSGRESSION

Adam was but human – this explains it all.
He did not want the apple for the apple's sake, he wanted it
only because it was forbidden. The mistake was in not
forbidding the serpent; then he would have eaten the serpent.[1]

Mark Twain, *Pudd'nhead Wilson*

## EVERYONE IS A SINNER

This book is about works of art that address a complicated subject: sin. Sins in a religious context are immoral acts that are considered transgressions against divine law. Sin also describes an aspect of the human condition in which we constantly fall short of the good. A sin in the secular world means something regarded as a serious or regrettable fault, offence or omission. Sin in this latter sense is immediately understandable: everyone at some point in their life commits a serious or regrettable fault, offence or fails to do the right thing. The concept that all human beings are necessarily sinful is one that has been discussed by early church figures, later theologians and even modern pop singers.[2] As Pet Shop Boys put it in their 1987 number 1 single *It's a sin*:

> Everything I've ever done
> Everything I ever do
> Every place I've ever been
> Everywhere I'm going to
> It's a sin[3]

If sin defines humankind, it must also define the art that humans create. Certainly sin has been the subject of countless works of art that have been made for centuries across the world. Just think of the many depictions of Adam and Eve eating forbidden fruit from the Tree of Knowledge, perhaps the most famous biblical story of them all. The term is also used more generally for something that is desired precisely because it is not allowed. Many pictures show us 'forbidden fruit' without a trace of the fruit mentioned in the Bible. Our notion of sin has been shaped by religious belief and doctrine, even though these roots are no longer always visible. One might say that these hidden roots are the roots of the Tree of Knowledge as described in the Book of Genesis. Of course there was already a concept of sin before the Old Testament was written.

Sin was there before the Christian Bible; indeed the concept more or less exists in all major world religions under different monikers. Judaism speaks of the *yetzer ha-ra*, the inclination to do evil and defy God. Islam mentions in the Quran (among many other concepts) *dhanb*, a concept very much like sin, and the concept of *haram* is used in Islam for things and acts that are forbidden. Actions that create negative karma are called *pāpa* in Hinduism, and Buddhism has *kilesa*, a form of moral corruption.[4] All these concepts are related to a general idea of sin, and they have informed a secularised and universally understood idea of 'good and bad' that we take for granted.

If sin indeed defines humankind, then writing a history of sin would entail writing a history of human beings: an impossible task. This story is largely about how artists have addressed one of art history's most defining and lasting subjects. It looks at paintings in the National Gallery – aided by a small number of external objects – through sin-tinted glasses, shedding new light on a great variety of works from the fourteenth to the twenty-first century. Because the National Gallery is a collection of paintings produced by artists working in Christian contexts, the story emphasises what Christianity has said and shown about sin, but the concerns, idiosyncrasies and ambiguities that arise from thinking about sin resonate far beyond these confines to other world religions and even to those of no faith. This overview deliberately moves back and forth between periods and countries. Sometimes it is specific and sometimes general to show how sin is universal (without wanting to be ahistorical). And besides it being universal, sin, paradoxically, can also be period-specific and deeply personal.

Before looking at paintings, this story starts with a drawing made by an artist who is well represented in the National Gallery's collection. It is one of the many drawings made by Sandro Botticelli to illustrate the medieval poet Dante's *Divina Commedia* (known in English as *The Divine Comedy*), an epic poem charting Dante's imaginary journey from

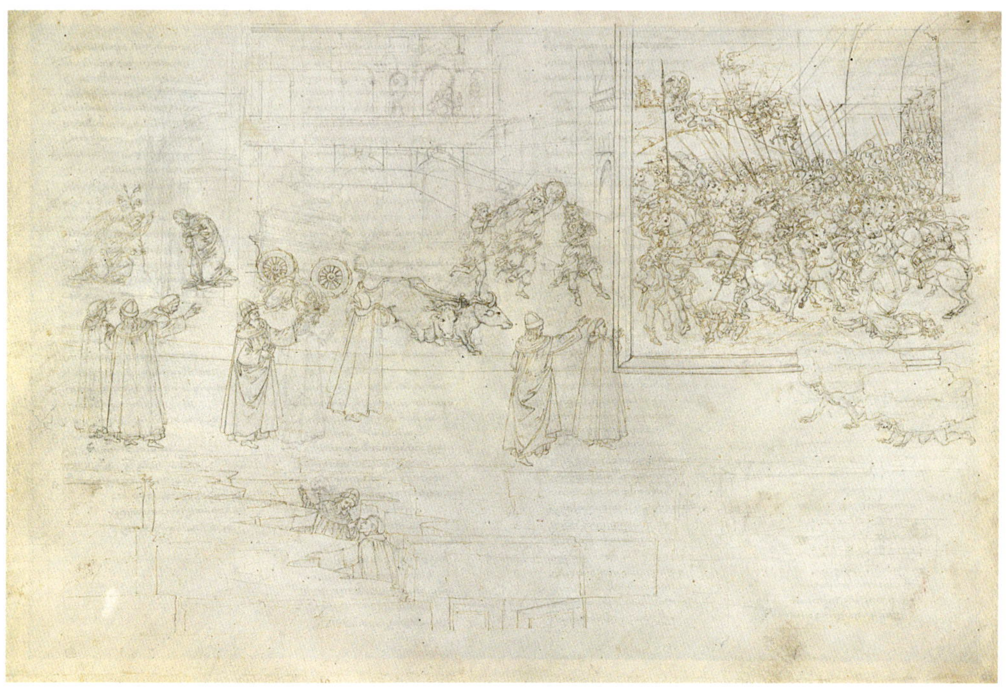

**1** Sandro Botticelli (about 1445–1510), *Purgatorio X: First Terrace: The Marble Carvings – Penance of the Proud*, 1490s. Drawing on parchment, 32 × 47 cm. Kupferstichkabinett, Staatliche Museen zu Berlin. Botticelli/cod. Hamilton 201

the depths of sin and evil in hell to the joys and blessings of heaven [1].[5] It is of course no coincidence that Dante's magnum opus makes an early appearance in our story about sin. The *Commedia*, and especially the section titled *Purgatorio*, is arguably literature's most emblematic exploration of sin and its consequences, in which sin is explained to Dante as being 'all acts deserving punishment'.[6]

Botticelli's drawing shows Dante and his guide, the classical Roman poet Virgil, in Purgatory, a place between heaven and hell which the Catholic Church believes to be inhabited by the souls of sinners who are working through and paying for their sins, a time of purification ahead of being admitted to heaven. The two poets enter through a narrow ravine and we see them move across a ledge, looking and pointing at three scenes. To the right, a pair of sinners crawl on all fours, carrying massive boulders on their backs. The metaphorical notion of sin as a weight or burden is here depicted literally.[7] Their particular sin is pride or, to give it its theological name in Latin, *superbia*, which is not only one of the seven deadly sins (see p. 38) but also regarded by some as the worst of the seven. Certainly the early and influential theologian, Saint Augustine, considered pride as the root of all other sins.[8] The three scenes that Dante and Virgil look at are identified as the Annunciation, the announcement of the Incarnation of Christ by the Archangel Gabriel to the Virgin Mary; David's Dance before the Ark of the Covenant, the moment the Old Testament king humbles himself before the holy Ark containing the tablets of Moses; and the Judgement of Emperor Trajan, where a poor widow halts the Roman emperor to plead vengeance for her murdered son. Apart from the Annunciation, the announcement of Christ's conception to the Virgin Mary, these may seem obscure episodes to us today, but theologians used them as examples of great humility. And the idea of humility is introduced in *Purgatorio X* as the antidote or corrective to pride. This explains why the sinners are not left carrying the weight of their sins unaided, but presented with examples of virtuous behaviour to speed up the working out of their sin. The three scenes of humility are in fact a 'gallery' of three works of art, 'effigies of true humility' carved in white marble.[9] Art historians love this particular drawing, because it shows works of art being not only beautiful but useful, as visual nourishment for the soul.[10]

It seems that Dante, and Botticelli following in his footsteps, considered works of art to be powerful enough to instil humility in these prideful sinners. Like Virgil and Dante in the epic poem and Botticelli's accompanying drawing, this book takes the reader on a journey through images. Although some of these images – mostly paintings – were meant to inspire virtuous behaviour, others are more complicated. Starting with pictures that address the earliest sin, this story explores 'sinful pictures' in which the 'art of transgression' comes to the fore, often blurring the boundaries between our modern categories, religious and secular, and showing how these pictures use ambiguity in a meaningful way. The journey continues by looking at (sometimes ambiguous) images of sins and sinful behaviour, before considering pictures that relate to humankind's attempts to do away with sin and to find redemption, and exploring Christ's role in sin. Ultimately, the works of art at the end of the journey prompt us to interrogate our own sins, as well as our ideas about sin.

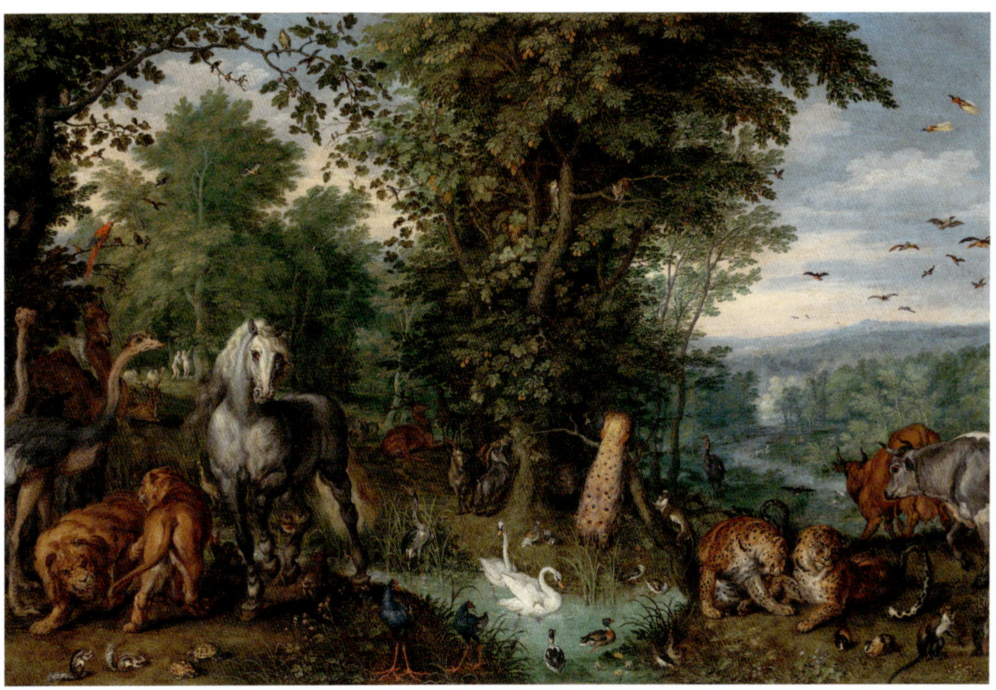

**2** Jan Brueghel the Elder (1568–1625), *The Garden of Eden*, 1613. Oil on copper, 23.7 × 36.8 cm. Private collection, Hong Kong, on long term loan to the National Gallery

## IN THE BEGINNING

The story of sin in art needs a beginning, and what could be more appropriate than the first book of the Christian Bible as well as part of the Jewish sacred texts, the Book of Genesis? Jan Brueghel the Elder's picture transports us to an unspoilt paradise, described in Genesis as the Garden of Eden [2]. Looking at this picture feels like intruding. The ostrich on the left, the camel, the prominent grey horse with its long flowing mane, the bear peeking from behind the tree and one of the leopards gaze out at us in a somewhat accusatory fashion. Their world seems in perfect harmony. The leopards lounge lazily, and not even the pair of lions causes any panic.

The abundant flora and fauna are not the full extent of this painting's subject. An essential detail lurks in the distance, framed by the ostrich's beak and the horse's mane. It is as if the painter wanted the 'intruding' viewer to take a moment to find a particular background

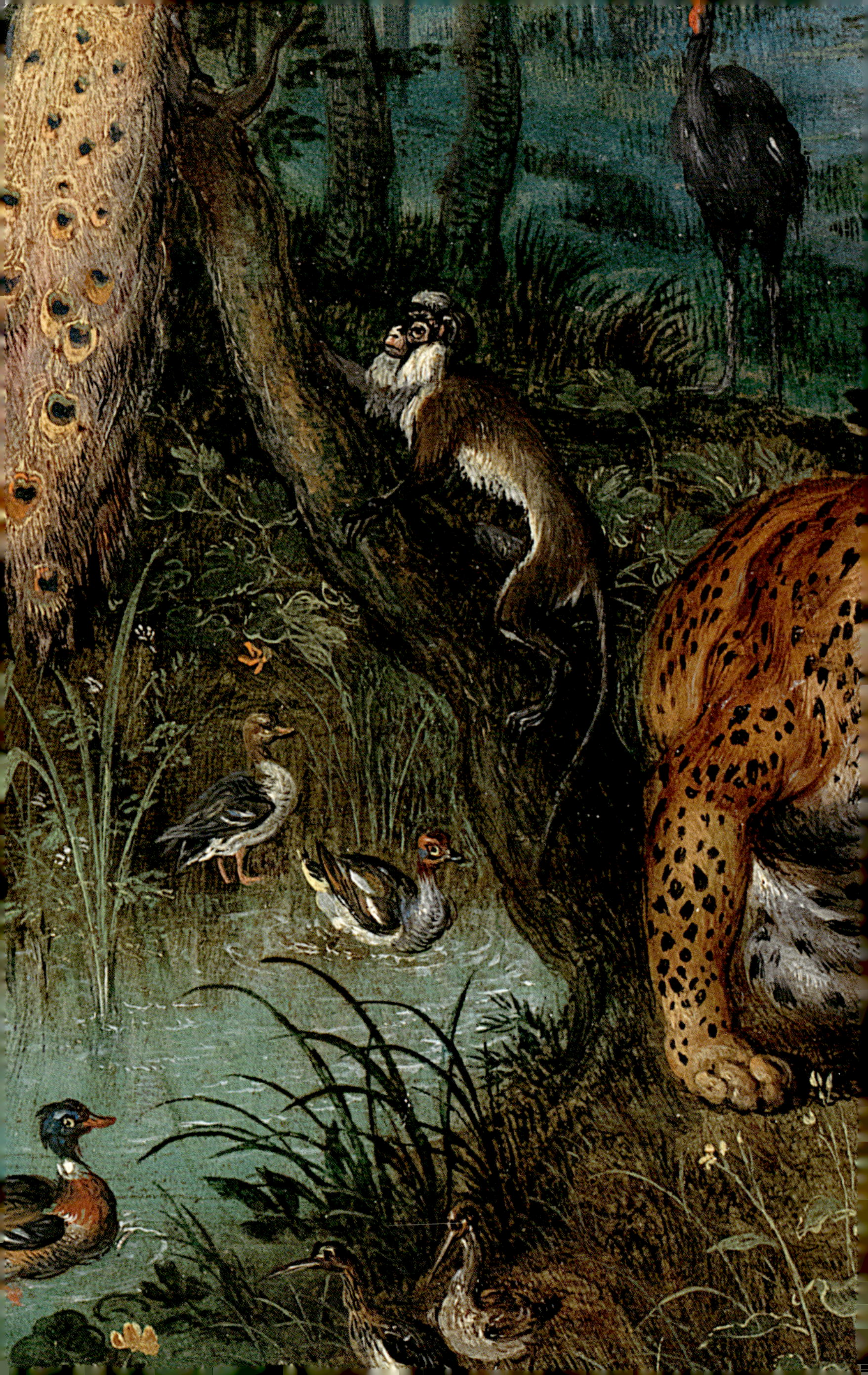

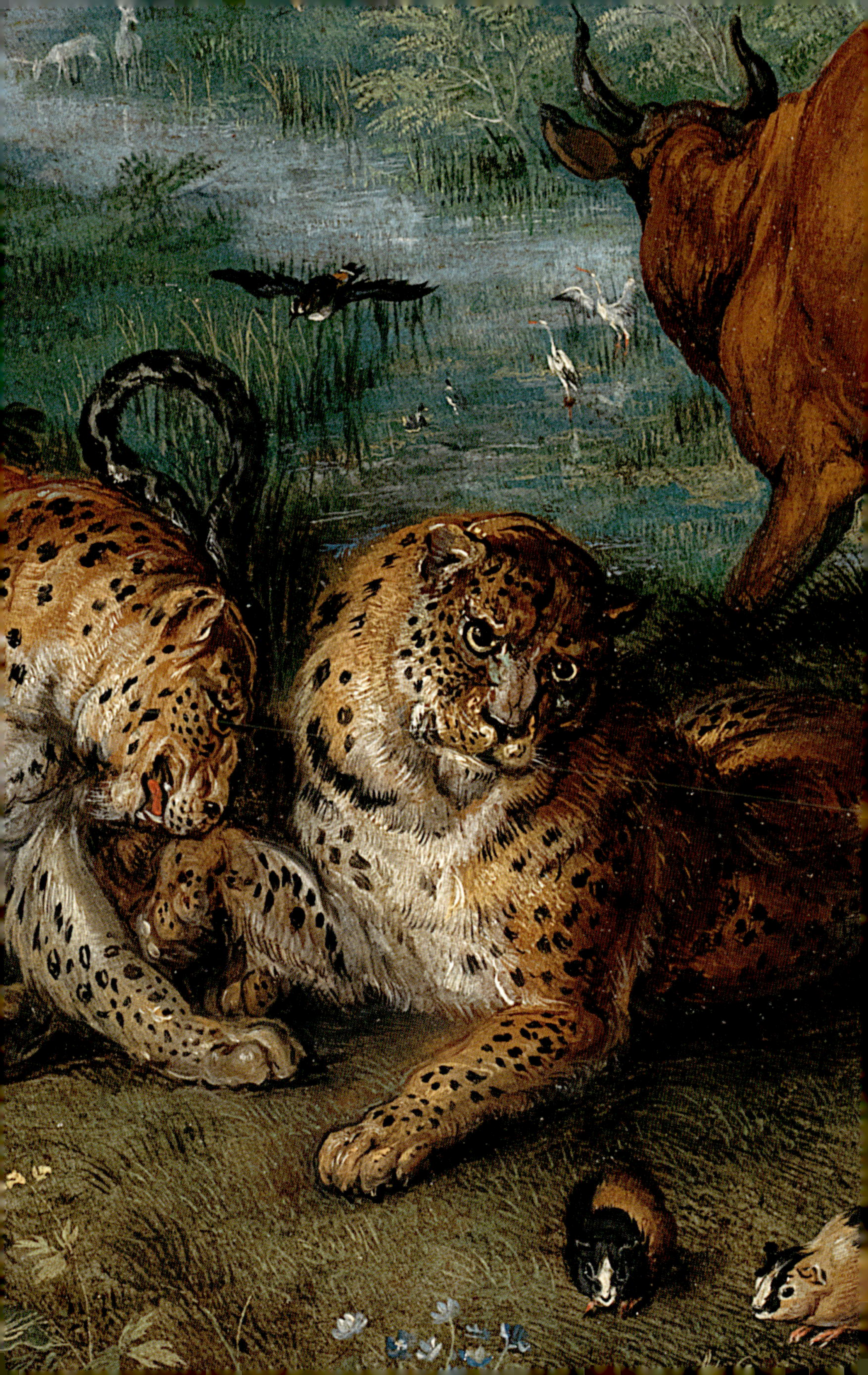

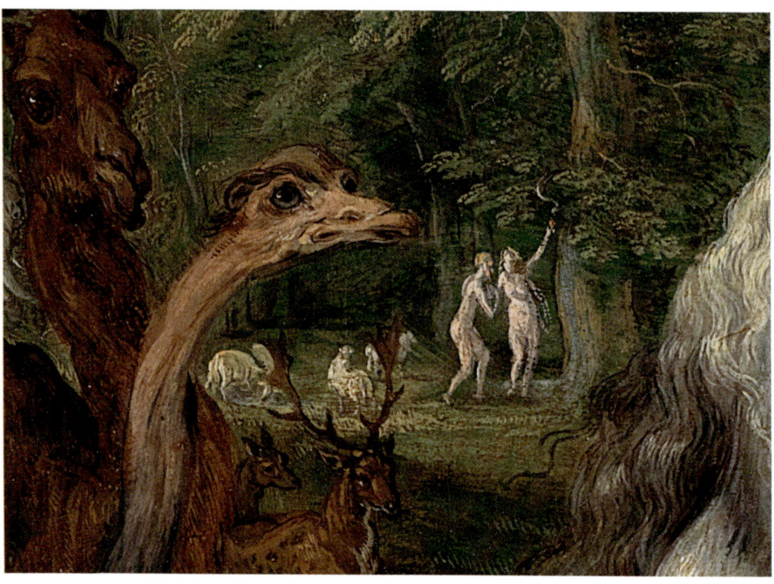

**3** (previous spread), **4** (above) Details from *The Garden of Eden*

detail. Given that the picture is so small, this detail is positively tiny [4]: two diminutive naked figures lit by a spotlight. The naked couple are Adam and Eve, who, according to the story in Genesis, were the first humans ever created and whose presence ensures that this is no ordinary animal-filled landscape. 'Paradise Brueghel' seems an appropriate nickname for the painter of these 'Paradise Landscapes'.[11] Brueghel painted a number of related works in which the Genesis narrative neatly unfolds in the background, starting in 1594, while in the service of the great patron of the arts Cardinal Federico Borromeo in Rome. Focusing on the couple in *The Garden of Eden* one can make out more details: the figure with the long hair must be Eve, and she raises her left arm to take some fruit. The second human figure, Adam, seems to be the recipient of fruit already plucked. The serpent is very inconspicuous, extending its body from a branch, almost touching the fruit. Of all the creatures, only the sheep looking up seems to notice what is going on.

However tiny Brueghel's detail may be, there is an inverse correlation between Adam and Eve's painterly scale and the scale of what they are embarking on. As far as stories go, that of Adam and

Eve is surely among the most enduring and potent.[12] It only takes up two pages of the Old Testament, but its legacy could fill the world's bookshelves. Depictions of Adam and Eve are everywhere, from illuminated manuscripts to fashion magazines.[13] Christians call this biblical account the 'Fall of Man'. In Genesis, chapter two, God places Adam in the Garden of Eden and permits him to eat from any tree, apart from the 'tree of the knowledge of good and evil'. God then proceeds to make a companion for Adam, Eve, who encounters a serpent in the third chapter of Genesis. The serpent asks Eve about the trees, and she replies that God specifically forbade eating from the Tree of Knowledge because that would mean certain death. The serpent challenges this, and Eve proceeds to eat fruit from the tree (the familiar apple is never specified!) and gives some to Adam too. All of a sudden, they are changed beings, ashamed of their nakedness – covering themselves with fig leaves and loincloths – and aware that they have acted in a way they should not have done, trying to hide from God. The first immoral act considered to be a transgression against divine law has been committed. *The Garden of Eden* already hints at the biblical story following Adam and Eve's sin, of the world's destruction and regeneration, as some of the animals already form distinct pairs that would join Noah (Adam's descendant) on the Ark [3]. But far beyond that, the first sin had grave consequences that would extend way beyond the flood narrative.

To understand these consequences we need to consider a complex but important theological concept: Original Sin. The doctrine of Original Sin teaches that a tendency towards evil is innate in all human beings, inherited from Adam in consequence of the Fall. The closest thing to a concept of Original Sin in the Bible is found in a letter of Saint Paul to the Romans (5: 18): 'Therefore just as one man's trespass led to condemnation for all, so one man's act of righteousness leads to justification and life for all.' Saint Augustine was the main thinker to develop this concept.[14] Lust is key in Augustine's theology theorising how Adam's sin was passed on from generation to generation, and by extension the human orgasm plays an important part. Augustine was not opposed to sex per se – indeed, he argued that sexual intercourse had a place before the Fall, and that in Eden orgasms were based on willpower and thus 'uncompromised' by sinful pleasure. But following the Fall self-serving pleasure takes over, and the mind cannot exercise rational judgement at the height of sexual excitement.[15] For Augustine, lust and self-love took the place of the love of God and the love of neighbour.

Perhaps one of the most famous depictions of the transgression that resulted in the idea of Original Sin is Lucas Cranach the Elder's *Adam and Eve* [5]. Cranach and his workshop completed at least 50 paintings of this subject.[16] In his 1526 painting Cranach brings to the fore what Jan Brueghel's later picture had placed in the background, namely the moment that Eve passes the fruit to Adam while the serpent looks on approvingly, willing them to commit their first sin. As in Brueghel's picture, the couple are surrounded by a menagerie of God's creation. What Cranach highlights is Adam's doubt in accepting the fruit. He scratches his curly head of hair with his left hand even as he accepts an apple with his right [6]. In some ways, Cranach's depiction of this pivotal moment is akin to the description of sin by the early English ecclesiastic, the Venerable Bede, in his once widely read *Ecclesiastical History* (completed in AD 731):

> For all sin is committed in three ways, namely by suggestion, pleasure, and consent. The devil makes the suggestion, the flesh delights in it and the spirit consents. It was the serpent who suggested the first sin, Eve representing the flesh was delighted by it, and Adam representing the spirit consented to it ...[17]

Adam seems to be actively consenting, and therefore the sin takes place. It is not the eating of the apple, but the agreeing to do so that makes the sin. And Adam's doubt is what makes the lofty subject so recognisable to all. Everyone is susceptible to sin, if they don't think too much about the consequences. Cranach painted in an intellectual environment that was increasingly shaped by the ideas of the great German sixteenth-century priest and theologian Martin Luther, which were instrumental in splitting the Church in half through the Protestant Reformation.[18] Luther's view of Adam's transgression is not dissimilar to Bede's, and emphasises how Adam's own will was instrumental in the story of sin.[19] Cranach's depiction of Adam scratching his head seems to draw attention to the manifestation of the sin in Adam's mind.

Close to Adam's head, the viper-like serpent lurking in the tree is not the only snake in Cranach's *Adam and Eve*. The painter's coat of arms, a winged serpent with a ring in its mouth, was granted to him

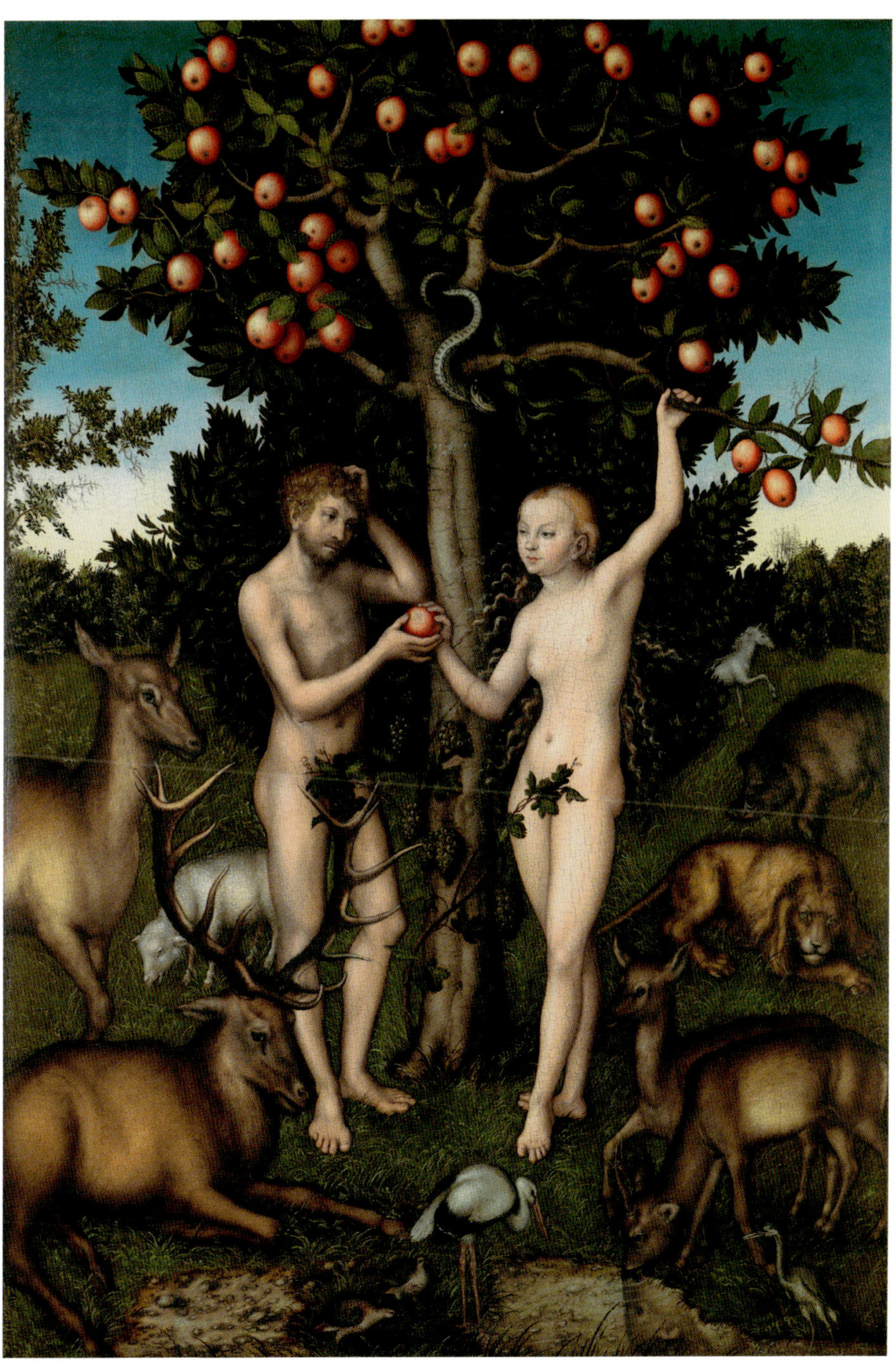

**5, 6** (detail, overleaf) Lucas Cranach the Elder (1472–1553), *Adam and Eve*, 1526. Oil on wood, 117.1 × 80.8 cm. The Samuel Courtauld Trust, The Courtauld Gallery, London on long term loan to the National Gallery

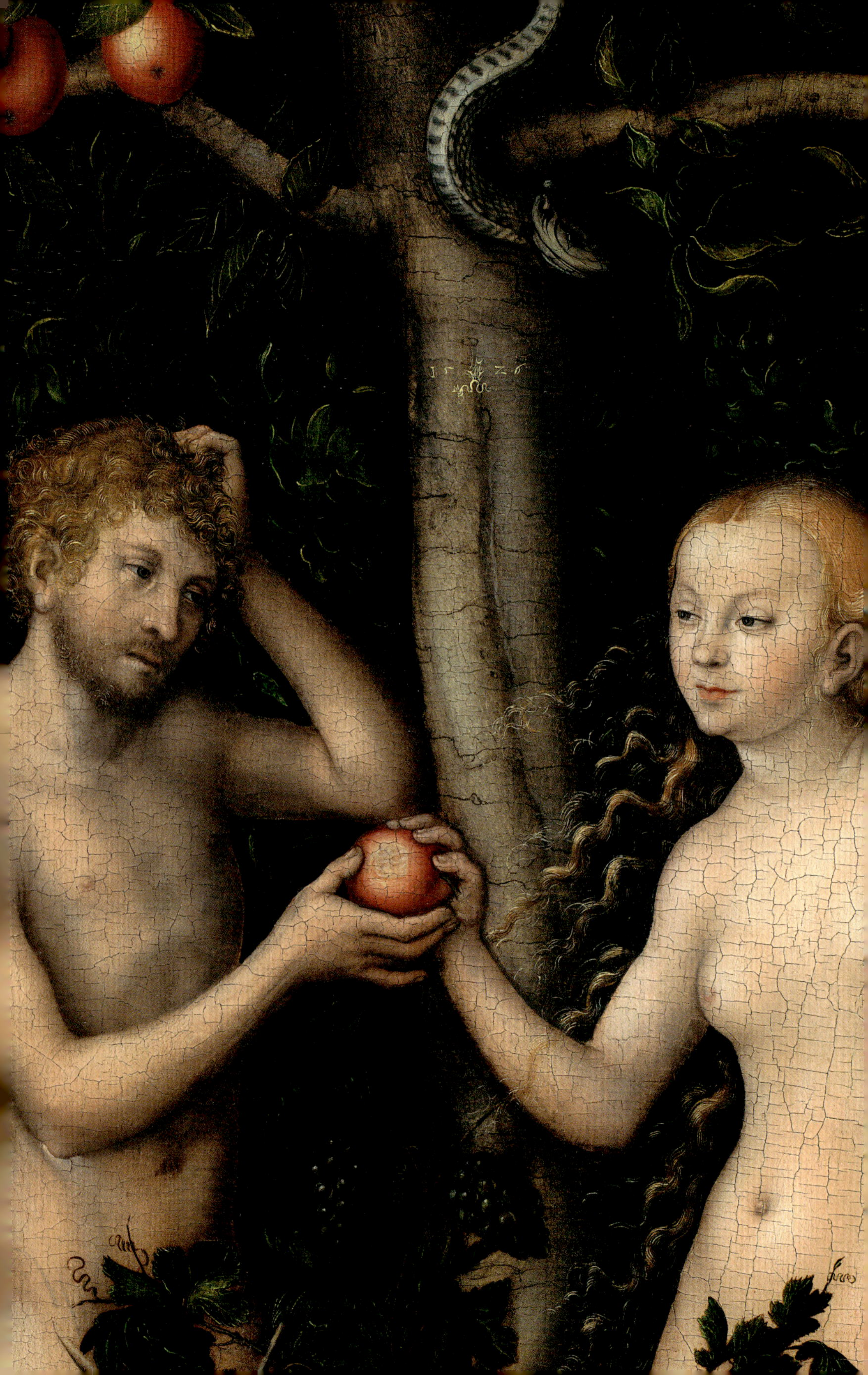

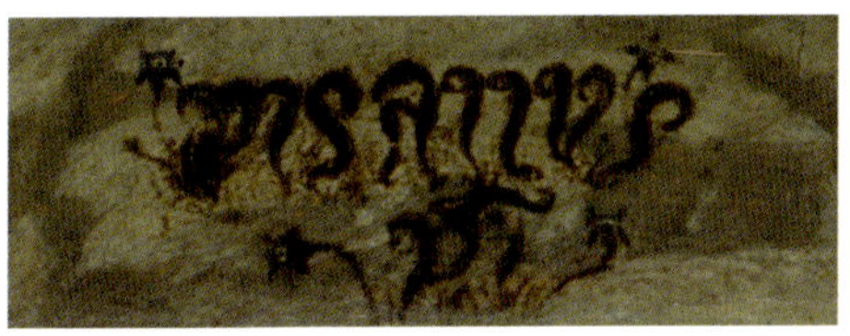

7 Detail of the artist's signature. Pisanello (about 1394?–1455), *The Virgin and Child with Saints*, about 1435–41. Egg tempera on poplar, 46.5 × 29 cm. The National Gallery, London

by Elector Frederick the Wise in 1508 and often appears as his signature [6].[20] The significance of the serpent signature is ambiguous and the combination of symbols conjures a variety of connotations. It has been suggested that Cranach's family name was in fact 'Sünder', the German word for sinner, although this hypothesis is no longer widely accepted.[21] The second serpent's location in *Adam and Eve* is striking nonetheless – on the bark just centimetres below the real serpent – as if Cranach is inscribing his own sinfulness on the Tree of Knowledge. To think of the artist using his signature as a 'self-conscious sinner' is not too much of a stretch. Looking at Pisanello's *Virgin and Child with Saints*, one art historian saw Pisanello's highly original signature as consisting of 'small snakes', self-consciously inscribing himself as a member of 'mankind under the curse of Original Sin' [7].[22] True or not, this is an intriguing observation, which links a possible interpretation of Pisanello's signature with Cranach's.

This art-historical anecdote about Pisanello's signature again brings Original Sin to the fore. While Augustine's concept affected Catholics and Protestants alike, there are important differences between the two when it comes to sin. Luther's followers believed in his maxim '*simul iustus et peccator*' ('simultaneously justified and sinner').[23] This means that man will always be a sinner and sin will not decrease, regardless of the fact that humans can simultaneously be treated as though they are righteous because of what Christ has done on their behalf (see p. 56). Catholics, however, believe that people are capable of 'decreasing' their sinful state, and affirm that moral effort contributes to a person's sanctification (their growing in holiness). Although there are many different ideas about sin, some of the basic aspects are fundamental for all Christians, Catholic or Protestant. One only needs to compare Brueghel's *Garden of Eden* with Cranach's *Adam and Eve*. The former originated in the decidedly Catholic environment of Cardinal Borromeo in Rome, while the latter was close to Luther. Both pictures emphasise the beauty and variety of God's creation and its flora and fauna, but even more, draw attention to the exact moment Eden's perfect harmony was lost and sin came into the world.

Adam and Eve's transgression had dire consequences, for themselves and for all human beings who came after them. The anonymous illuminator of the so-called *Holkham Bible Picture Book* depicted the first sin and its aftermath on a single folio with great ingenuity [8]. The manuscript was made in London in the early fourteenth century for a Dominican friar and contains only a few key sections of the Bible: the stories of the origin of the world from Genesis to Noah, the Gospels and the Book of Revelation, describing the end of the world.[24] As its name suggests, the *Picture Book* tells the story of sin predominantly through imagery. The page in question, which illustrates the final sentence of Genesis 3, depicts the shame felt by Adam and Eve as they crouch and cover up their genitals. A perhaps surprising detail in the illumination is that the serpent is depicted with a human head, something that originated with the emergence of mystery plays – which included re-enactments of the story of Adam and Eve – from the thirteenth century onwards.[25] Another noteworthy detail is the look of utter distress on Adam's face as an angel brandishing a sword chases the couple out of Eden's gate in the Expulsion of Adam and Eve. Recent neuroscientific research measured the brain activity of a group of people observing three different paintings. The test showed the strongest response came from those looking at a picture of the Expulsion from Paradise.[26] It seems the depiction of being forcefully removed from an earthly paradise, never to return, provokes strong reactions. Both the illuminator and the patron of the *Holkham Bible Picture Book* seem to have understood that pictures speak louder than words.

Not only Adam and Eve, but the serpent too was punished for its part in the first sin: 'Because you have done this, cursed are you among all animals and among all wild creatures; upon your belly you shall go, and dust you shall eat all the days of your life.' (Genesis 3: 15) Although Jan Gossaert's small panel depicts two characters from the New Testament [9] – the Virgin Mary and the infant Christ – the words that frame them are borrowed from God's address to the snake in the Old Testament's Genesis story: 'I will put enmity between you

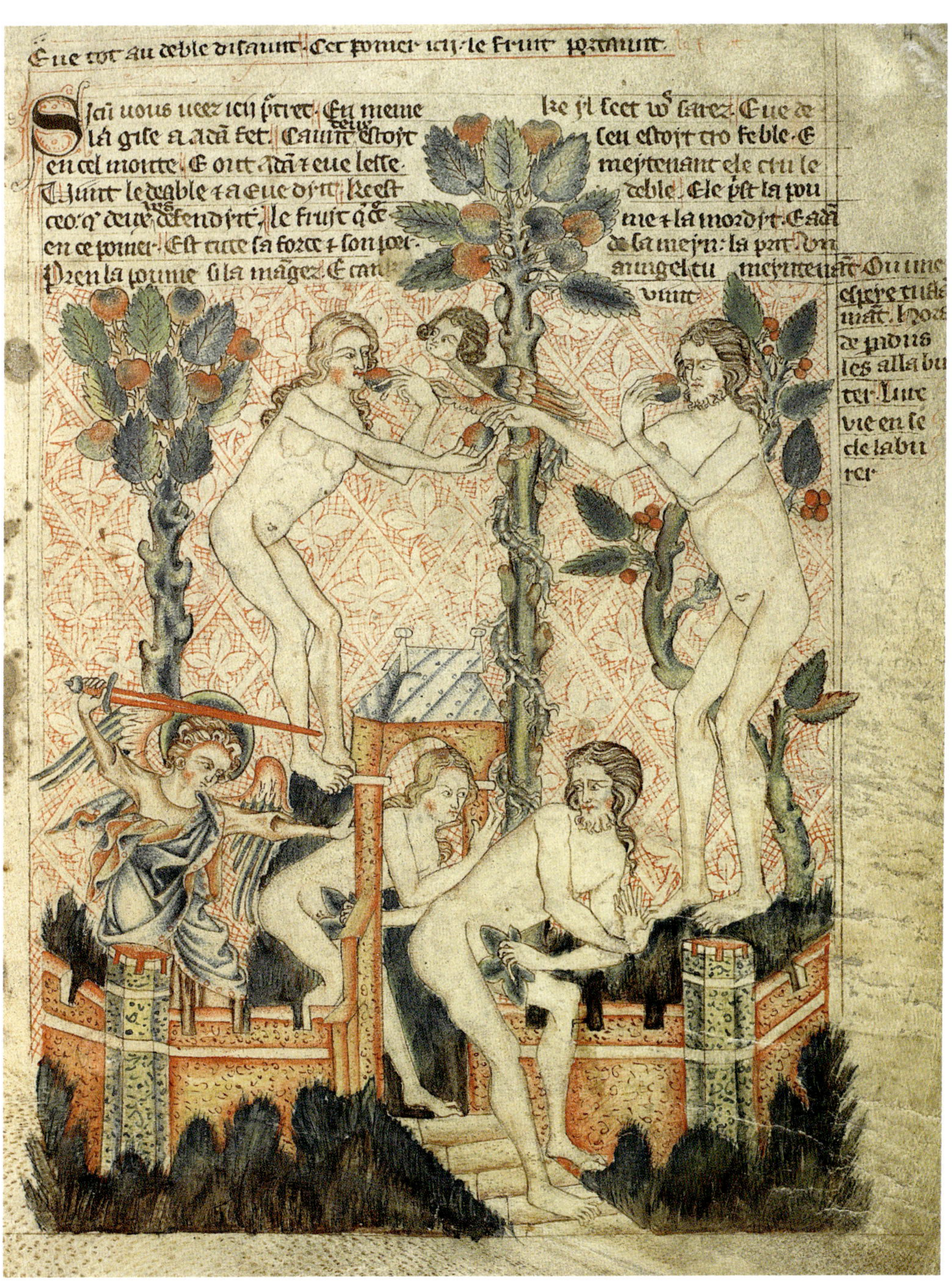

**8** Anonymous Anglo-Norman illuminator, *Bible (the 'Holkham Bible Picture Book')*, folio 4, *The Transgression and Expulsion*, about 1327–35. Parchment codex, 28.5 × 21 cm. The British Library, London. Add MS 47682

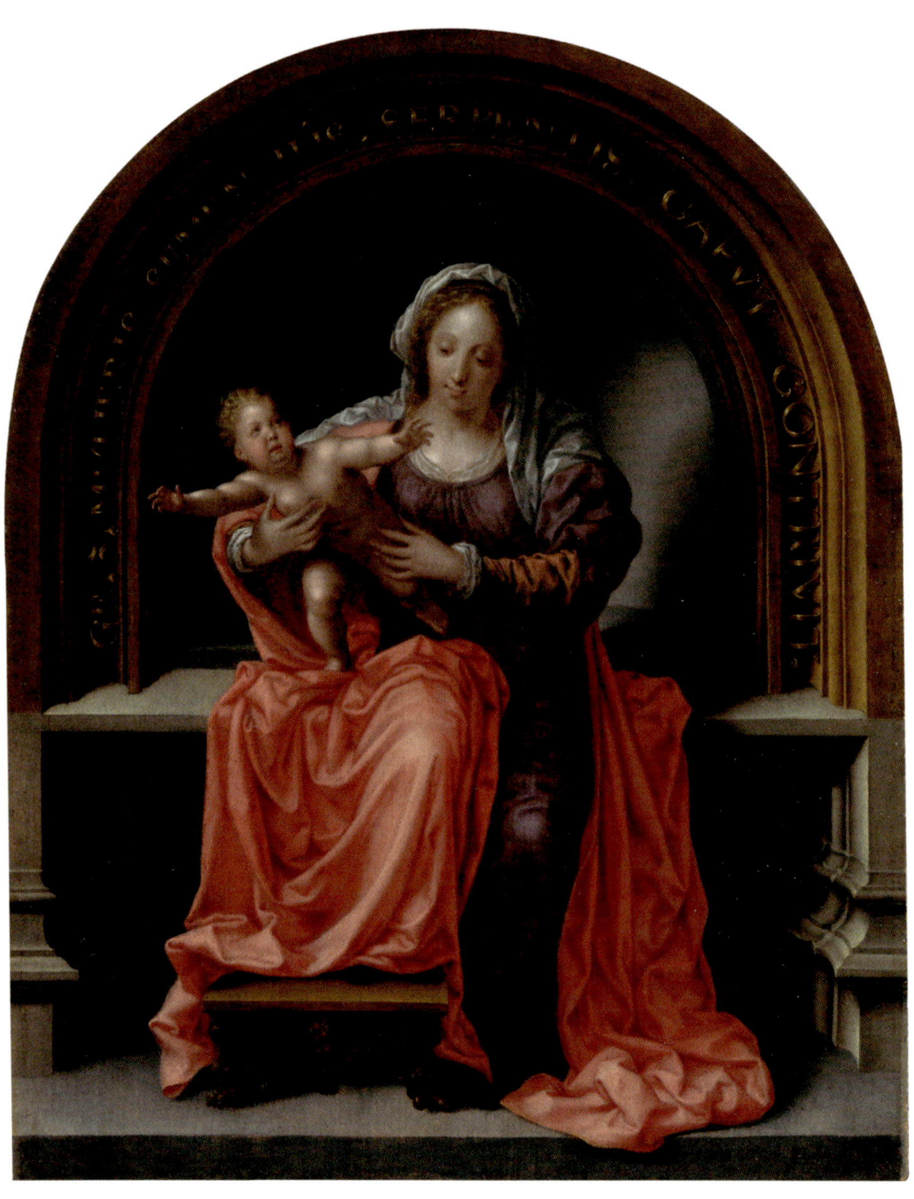

**9** Jan Gossaert (Jean Gossart) (active 1508; died 1532),
*The Virgin and Child*, 1527. Oil on oak, 30.7 × 24.3 cm. The National Gallery, London

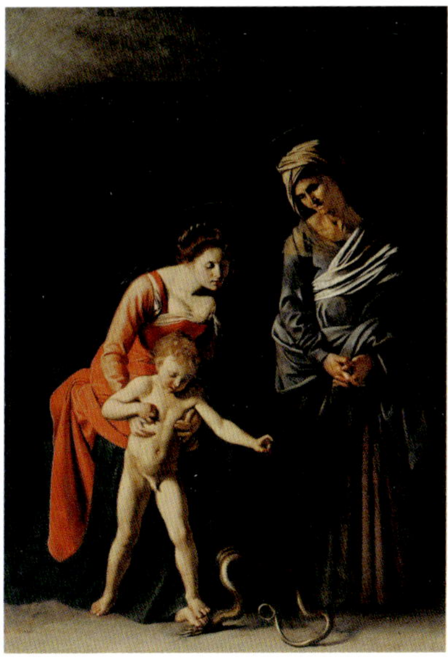

**10** Michelangelo Merisi da Caravaggio (1571–1610), *Madonna and Child with Saint Anne ('Madonna dei Palafrenieri')*, 1605–6. Oil on canvas, 292 × 211 cm. Galleria Borghese, Rome

and the woman, and between your offspring and hers; he will strike your head, and you will strike his heel'. We can translate Gossaert's inscription as: 'The seed of the woman has bruised the head of the serpent.'[27] In the same passage where Saint Paul referenced an idea of Original Sin, he developed the idea expressed here of Christ being the enemy of evil (Romans 5: 18): 'Therefore just as one man's trespass led to condemnation for all, so one man's act of righteousness leads to justification and life for all', the latter 'one man' being Christ. The Christ Child in Gossaert's painting seems ready for action, as he springs from his mother's lap. Arms outstretched, he appears to prefigure his own crucifixion. Christians believe that Christ's death on the Cross restored the relationship between God and humanity (see p. 56). Furthermore, the Virgin's throne looks an awful lot like an altar, the kind of altar on which Christ's sacrifice would be re-enacted in the Eucharist.

In the following century Caravaggio took the Genesis 3 inscription from Gossaert's picture a step further in his painted depiction of 'the seed of the woman' punishing the snake.[28] The *Madonna and Child with Saint Anne*, also known as the *Madonna dei Palafrenieri* [10], was made for the altar of the Archconfraternity of the Papal Grooms in the Vatican Basilica of Saint Peter. It conveys a sophisticated theological argument in the apparent guise of an intimate family moment. Mary helps her toddler son with his first steps as her own mother looks on, Christ's right foot tenderly placed on his mother's. The familiarity ends there, because mother and son are trampling on a snake, just as God foretold in Genesis. Caravaggio's cleverness lies in showing Mary as 'co-redeemer'.[29] A contemporary sonnet on the painting by the Roman jurist Marzio Milesi celebrates the picture's hopeful message and Caravaggio's ingenuity:

> On account of Adam's sin miserable humanity strayed in anger from its maker, but when God was made man, humankind was reborn, and hoped [the Saviour] would reopen for it the path to heaven. Whence that serpent who was the cause of original sin was trampled down and oppressed by the mother and the son ...[30]

## EVE/VENUS: AN INTRODUCTION TO AMBIGUITY

Up until now the Genesis story of Adam and Eve and its aftermath have loomed large. There is, however, an important aspect in some of these images that has hitherto not been addressed outright: ambiguity. Although these pictures might seem overtly moralising to some, warning the viewer about the repercussions of Adam and Eve's actions, a viewer unaware of the Book of Genesis may perceive something else. Let us look at Cranach's *Adam and Eve* again [5]. It is a picture of the Fall, the heat of the moment of the first sin, but also an image of a beautiful naked man and woman in a lush green landscape, surrounded by the bounty of creation. This is a picture to be enjoyed, and maybe even one that excites and arouses. It is moralising but also seductive, although one does not exclude the other. It certainly allows us to enjoy the human body, or even to lust after that body. Yet lust is a sin. Can a picture that warns us of sin concurrently inspire sin? What if, to the detriment of Augustine and his concept of Original Sin, lust takes over, and the mind loses control?

In addition to his many Eves, Cranach also painted a large number of Venuses. His depictions of the first woman in Genesis and the Goddess of Love from Roman mythology often look similar.[31]

The National Gallery owns two prime examples of the latter. *Cupid complaining to Venus* [12] was painted about the same time as *Adam and Eve*, and *Venus and Cupid* [11] just afterwards. Both smaller in size, their subject is surprisingly alike. In these three pictures, Venus and Eve are almost interchangeable on account of shared formal qualities. Apart from the presence of Adam in the image of Eve, one would be hard-pressed to tell the difference [13]. The writer and artist John Berger summarised the bigger issue in his *Ways of Seeing*: 'You painted a naked woman because you enjoyed looking at her, put a mirror in her hand and you called the painting "Vanity," thus morally condemning the woman whose nakedness you had depicted for your own pleasure.'[32] The same could easily be said for Cranach's Eve/Venus. What does it mean that Eve looks like Venus and Venus like Eve?[33]

*Cupid complaining to Venus* very explicitly plays on the Eve trope, as Venus grasps the branch of an apple tree.[34] Meanwhile, her son Cupid complains that he has been stung by bees after stealing a honeycomb. His desire for honey has led to trouble, and maybe the viewer's desire leads down a similar path. Cranach signed the work with his customary winged serpent with a ring in its mouth, not on the tree this time, but on a rock above which Venus' foot seductively hovers. *Venus and Cupid* is similar in many ways. Whereas the former Venus is completely nude, in this picture a translucent veil plays with the suggestion of covering up, although her nakedness is fully on display. No fig leaves and loincloths here. The two *Venuses* were most likely made for private spaces, whereas the almost equally naked Eve in Cranach's *Adam and Eve* might have been considered a more pious picture.

The beauty of painting is that it allows a certain open-endedness – one could even call it 'deniability' – that a written text may not;[35] a useful ambiguity that allows a picture to be many things at once. It was not only Cranach and his patrons who used this to their advantage. We also see this ambiguity at play in two further pictures by Gossaert: an *Adam and Eve* [15] and another mythological subject, *Hercules and Deianira* [14]. Although the latter is based on a story from Ovid's *Metamorphoses* (a collection of mythological tales) and the picture is much smaller, its protagonists, Hercules and his wife Deianira, look almost interchangeable with the couple from the Genesis story. Gossaert, like Cranach, painted many *Adam and Eves*: he made this one around 1520 and the *Hercules and Deianira* just before that in 1517.

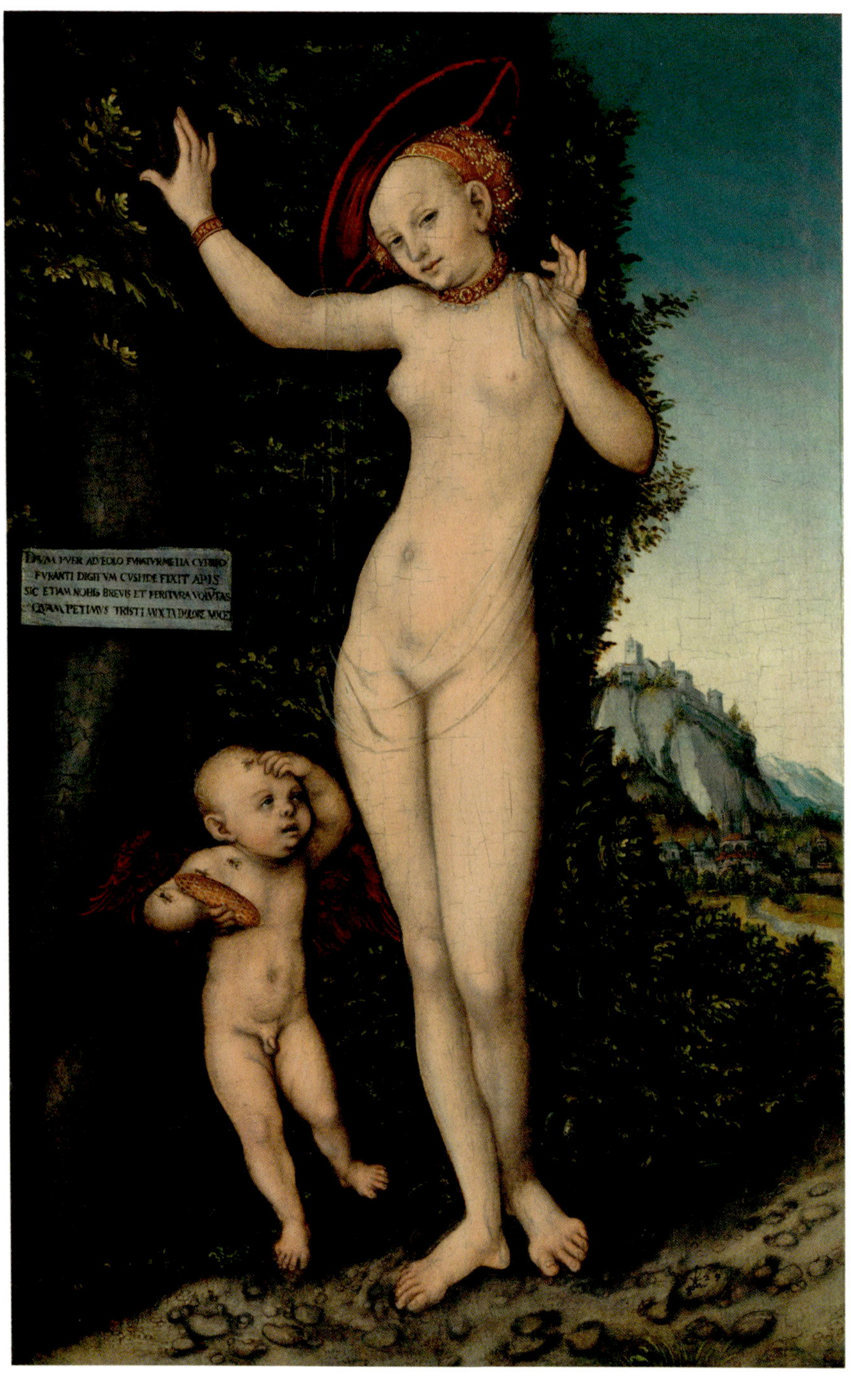


**11** Lucas Cranach the Elder (1472–1553), *Venus and Cupid*, 1529.
Oil on wood, 38.1 × 23.5 cm. The National Gallery, London

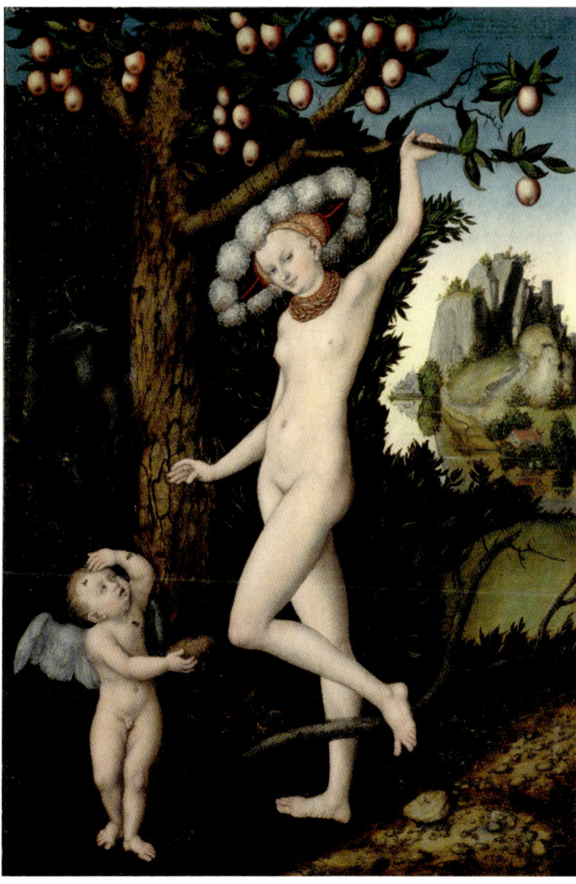

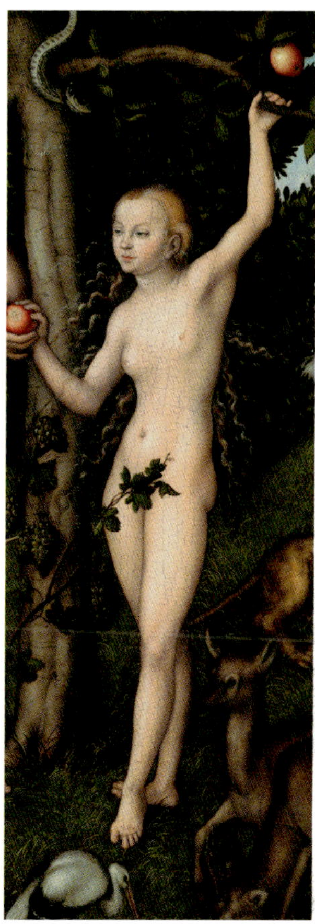

**12** Lucas Cranach the Elder (1472–1553), *Cupid complaining to Venus*, 1526–7. Oil on wood, transferred to masonite, 81.3 × 54.6 cm. The National Gallery, London

**13** Detail of Eve from *Adam and Eve*, p. 19

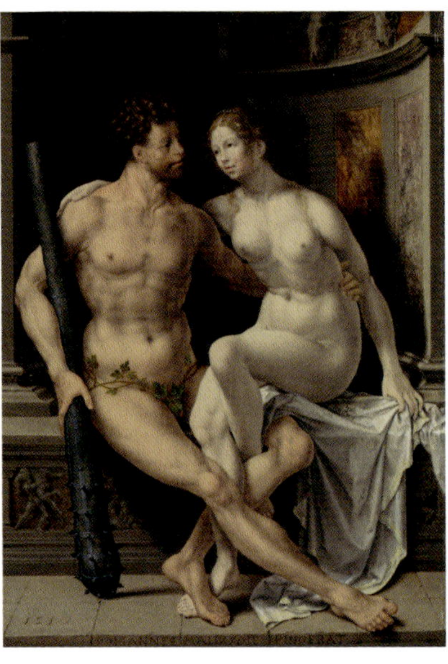

**14** Jan Gossaert (Jean Gossart) (active 1508; died 1532), *Hercules and Deianira*, 1517. Oil on oak, 36.8 × 26.6 cm. The Barber Institute of Fine Arts, Birmingham

The latter has been interpreted in the light of female sexual power over men.[36] Hercules seems to have inherited Adam's fig leaves, but the largely nude couple's entangled legs and intent gazes convey sexuality. Without wanting to close down the comparison too much, both Gossaert's pictures again appear to play on a meaningful ambiguity. The boundaries between pictorial morality and seductive sinfulness seem remarkably fluid.

## THE ART OF TRANSGRESSION

Bronzino's eccentric picture of *An Allegory with Venus and Cupid* could be described as the 'anti-Virgin and Child' [16]. While it combines many familiar elements that have already featured in this story, most notably a divine mother and child, its subjects here are Venus and Cupid instead of Mary and Jesus.[37] As in the two paintings by Cranach discussed earlier, an apple features prominently, but this one is made of gold and held by Venus. Although it is the apple presented to her by Paris as the most beautiful of all goddesses, one is immediately reminded of Eve,

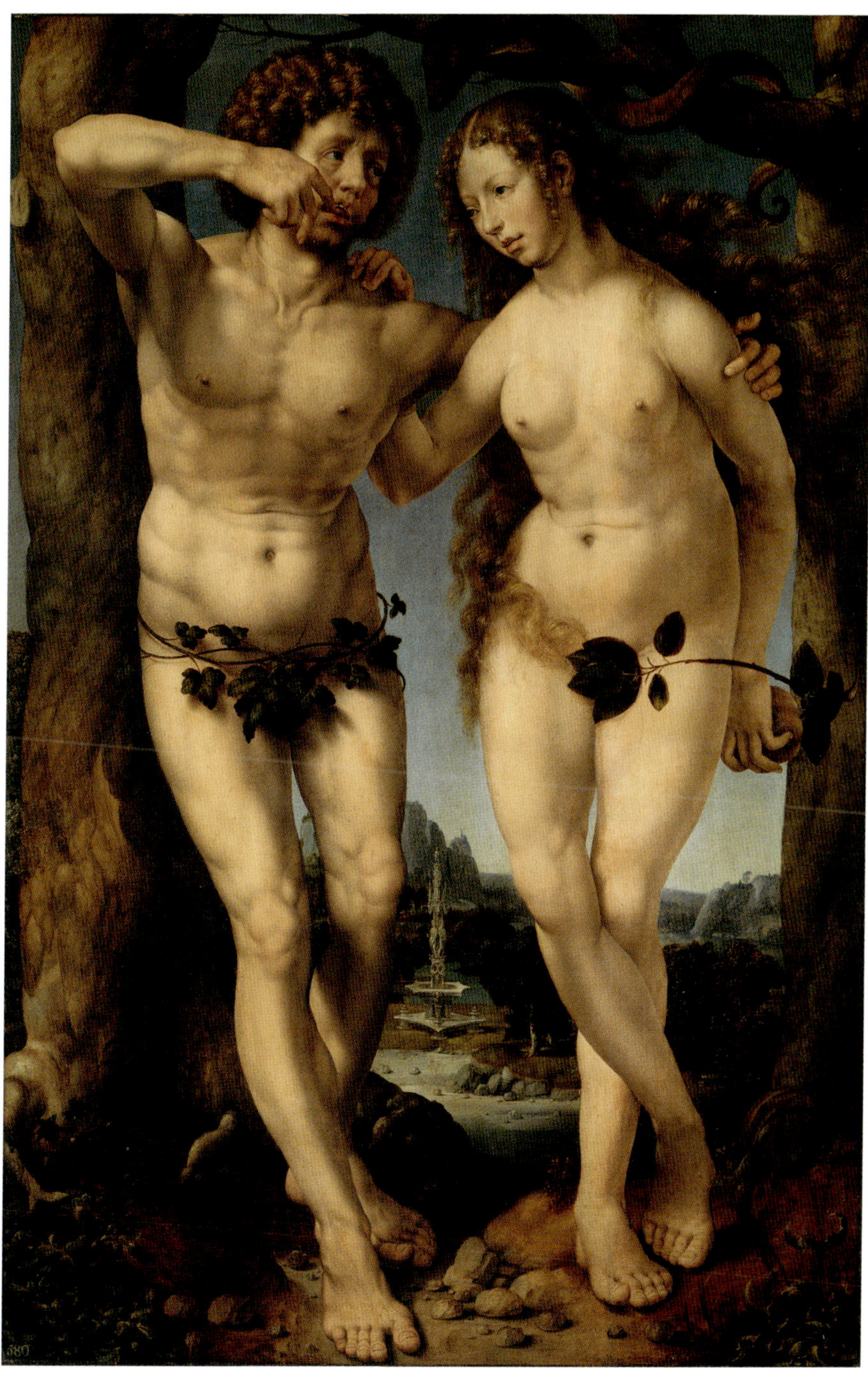

**15** Jan Gossaert (Jean Gossart) (active 1508; died 1532), *Adam and Eve*, about 1520.
Oil on wood, 168.9 × 111.4 cm. On long term loan from
Her Majesty the Queen to the National Gallery

all the more because of the figure with the serpent-like lower body lurking in the shadows behind her, offering a honeycomb just as Cupid does in Cranach's pictures. This serpentine figure also recalls the 'snake' in the Tree of Knowledge in the *Holkham Bible Picture Book* [see 8]. This does not mean, however, that this painting is presented in this story as an 'allegory of sin' employing protagonists from classical antiquity and subtle allusions to the story of Adam and Eve. The last thing that Bronzino's *Allegory* needs is another iconographic analysis. The picture remains puzzling. Giorgio Vasari, the sixteenth-century artist and biographer, describes it (or a closely related picture) briefly in his *Lives of the Artists*, and his description is still the basis for how we interpret the picture today:

> ... he painted a picture of singular beauty that was sent to King Francis in France, wherein was a nude Venus with a Cupid who was kissing her, and Pleasure on one side with Play and other Loves, and on the other side Fraud and Jealousy and other passions of love.[38]

Many art historians have attempted to 'decipher' Bronzino's picture, although there is no definitive answer to the puzzle.[39] Its complexity makes even a short description challenging: Venus steals an arrow from her son Cupid as she passionately kisses him. Cupid, in turn, fondles Venus' breast. His buttocks are provocatively on show as he attempts to steal his mother's crown [17]. The masks at her feet suggest that she and Cupid exploit lust to mask deception. The howling figure on the left could be Jealousy/Envy. The boy scattering roses and stepping on a thorn could be Folly or Pleasure. The serpentine creature already mentioned is often interpreted as a personification of Fraud or Deceit. In the background, Father Time vies with a mask-like personification of Oblivion to either reveal or conceal the enigmatic scene. 'Allegorical' is often used to describe pictures whose meaning eludes us, and Bronzino's *Allegory* is a case in point. It is a conversation piece first and foremost, something that appealed to an elevated court culture animated by learned games. Its visual riddles and erudite allusions warrant attention and invite speculation. Probably not even Bronzino and his patron Francis I could 'explain' the picture and all its riddles. Looking at it and attempting to describe it does make clear

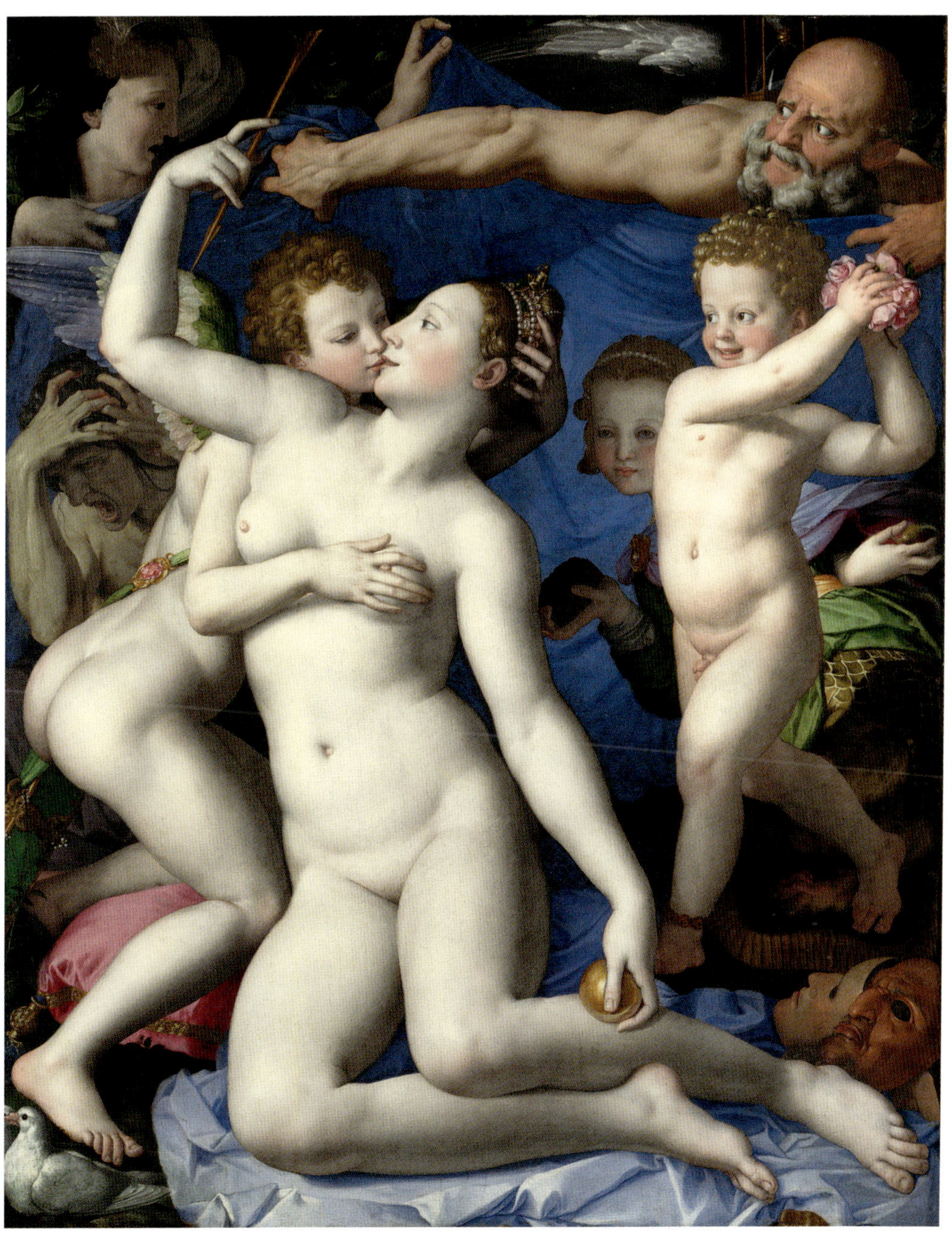

**16, 17** (detail, overleaf) Bronzino (1503–1572), *An Allegory with Venus and Cupid*, about 1545. Oil on wood, 146.1 × 116.2 cm. The National Gallery, London

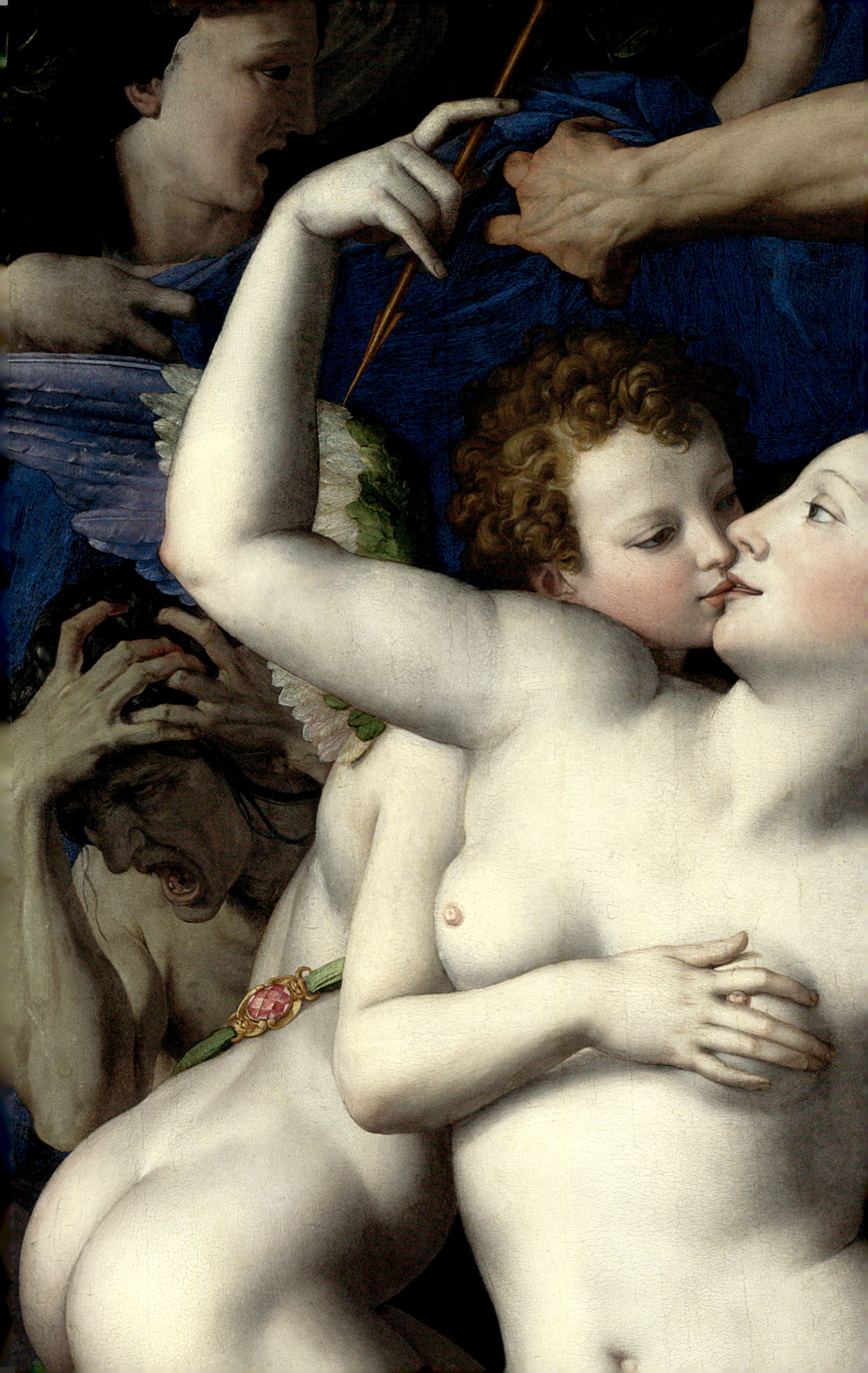

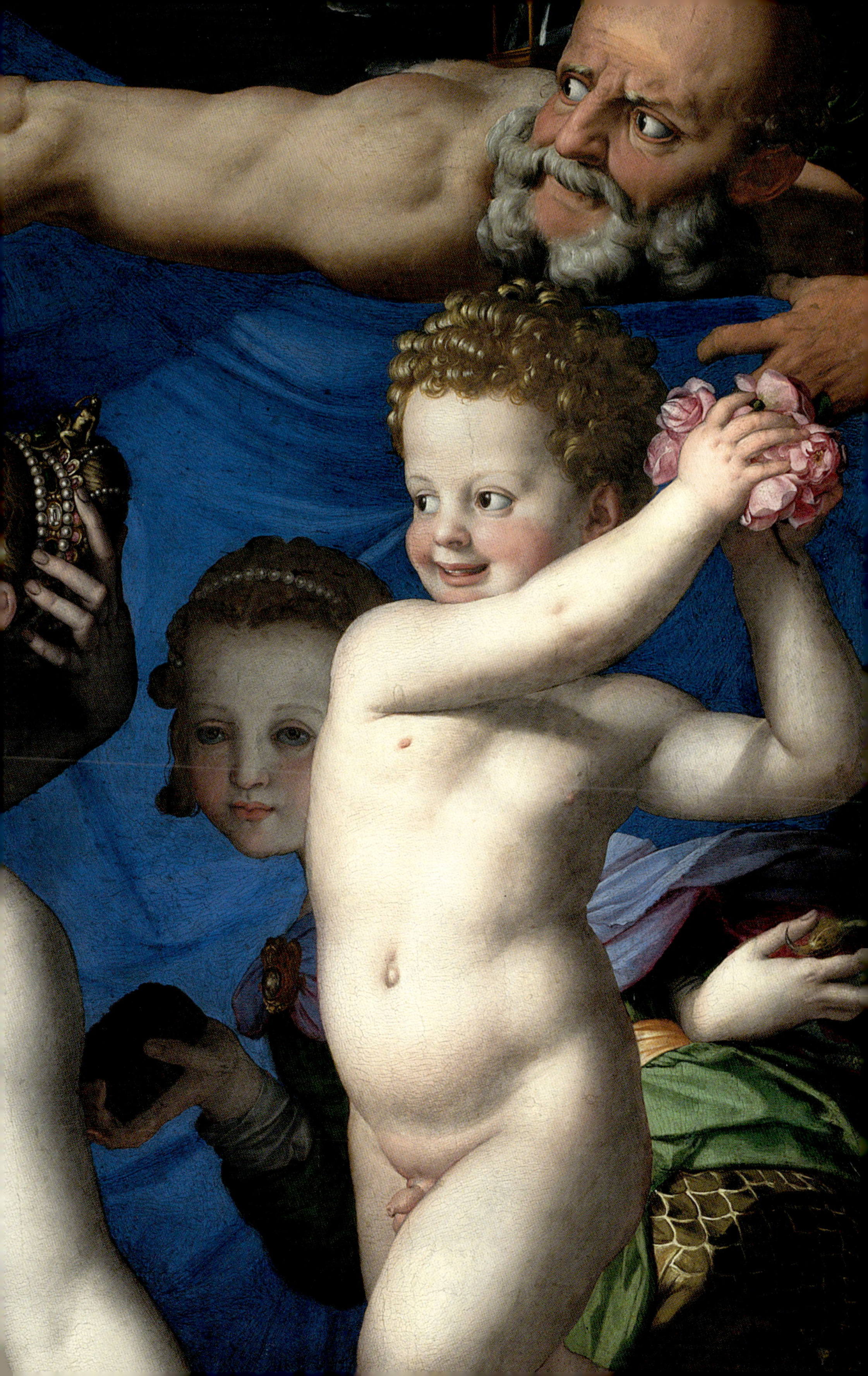

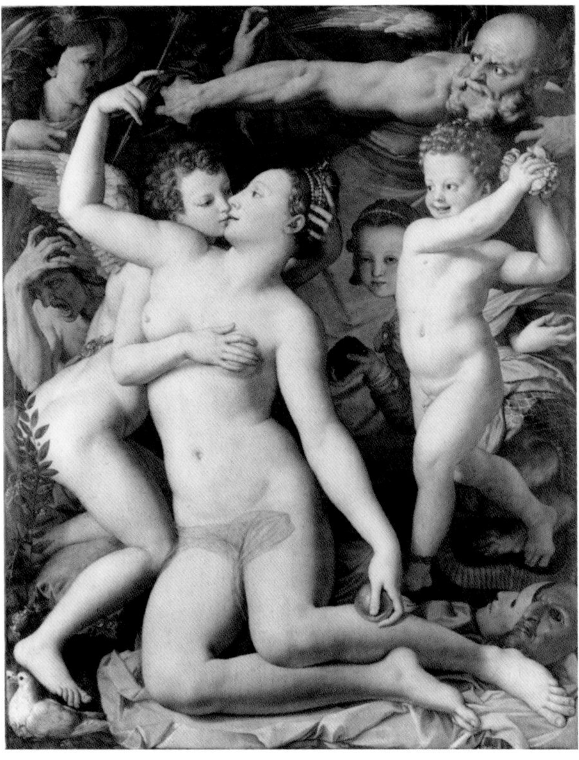

**18** Bronzino, *An Allegory with Venus and Cupid*, about 1545. Photograph pre-1958 restoration.

that it is a very sexual picture, a sinful one even.[40] One of the more interesting examples of art historians attempting to decipher it must surely be the painting's association with syphilis, as the figure clutching its head behind Cupid seems to be displaying some of the symptoms of this sexually transmitted disease.[41]

One can only imagine how this picture would have been received by an audience beyond the court of Francis I at Fontainebleau and Bronzino's artistic circles. What we do know, however, is how the picture was received at Trafalgar Square. Already in its early history during the reign of Louis XIV, 'flimsy lingerie' was added to hide Venus' genitalia and myrtle was painted over Cupid's prominent buttocks.[42] When the National Gallery's first director Sir Charles Eastlake acquired the picture from the Beaucousin collection in Paris in 1860, he wrote to the Gallery's Keeper that its former owner considered the Bronzino 'the most

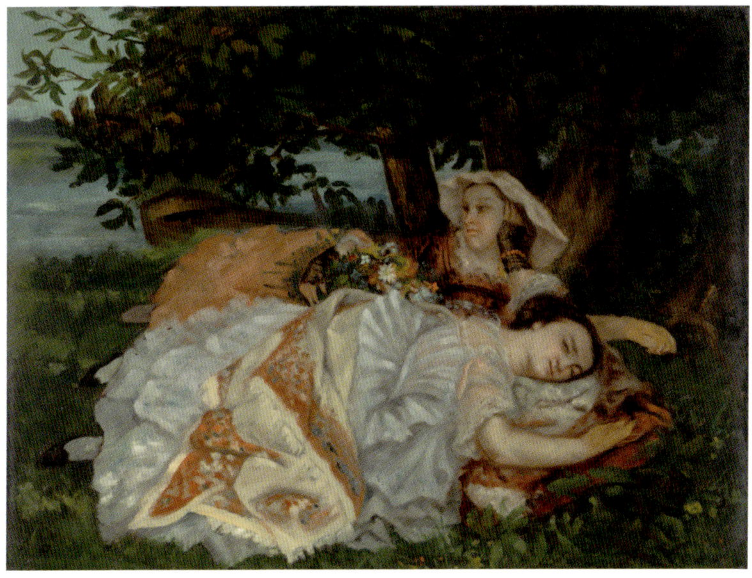

**19** Possibly after Gustave Courbet (1819–1877), *Young Ladies on the Banks of the Seine (Summer)*, possibly 1870s. Oil on canvas, 96.5 × 130 cm. The National Gallery, London

improper picture', and that Monsieur Beaucousin had always covered the painting with a veil.[43] Eastlake instructed a restorer to conceal Venus' tongue entering her son's mouth and to remove the erect nipple between Cupid's groping fingers, adding to the 'restorations' done under Louis XIV [18].[44] Eastlake also added the Bronzino to the top of a list labelled 'superfluous pictures' that were meant to be sent on loan to the National Gallery of Scotland (although it never left London).[45] While the *Allegory* was clearly considered too much for the prudish Victorian public, the picture was finally restored to its original state in 1958.[46]

If the institutional history of Bronzino's *Allegory* seems particular to Victorian morals, one only needs to cross the Channel to find a contemporaneous example in which a picture closely related to one in the National Gallery was condemned for its eroticism. Possibly painted after Gustave Courbet, the National Gallery's *Young Ladies on the Banks of the Seine (Summer)* [19] seems positively pedestrian to a modern viewer in comparison to Bronzino's sexual indiscretions between the mythical mother and son.[47] However, its subject caused a scandal when a larger version of the scene painted by Courbet (Musée du Petit Palais, Paris) appeared at the Paris Salon in 1857. Picturing two young ladies of leisure lounging on the riverbank was a provocative subject according to the critics – they were clearly prostitutes! – and one could even see what was then considered their underwear.[48] Linda Nochlin has since uncovered and effectively dismantled the hypocrisy of such 'misogynistic and moralistic' outrage, but the critics' 1857 sentiment remains as a historical document of such attitudes to pictures.[49]

It seems from the outline of Bronzino's ambiguous but sexually charged subject and its critical fortune and institutional afterlife, as well as our brief look at Courbet's Paris in 1857, that all sorts of paintings end up being about sin and sinfulness, often both in conception and reception. It often does not matter if they show religious subject matter. Certainly, examples of what we call the seven deadly sins, capital vices or cardinal sins have featured in this story already, both explicitly and implicitly, and they appear both in religious and non-religious contexts. This group of the seven worst sins is probably what most people think of when they hear the word 'sin'. There is something orderly about their number, and each conjures evocative imagery: pride, greed, lust, envy, gluttony, wrath and sloth.

The list was standardised by the sixth-century pope, Gregory I (Saint Gregory the Great) in his commentary on the Old Testament Book of Job, *Moralia in Job*.[50] Other 'standardised' lists were produced, but Gregory's proved the most authoritative in the long run.[51] Many artists over the centuries have sought to give visual expression to the seven deadly sins. An excellent example is the *Table of the Seven Deadly Sins* made by Hieronymus Bosch (or his workshop), which gathers many of the themes found in these pages in a single object. All of the standard seven sins are depicted in a neat circle, around a risen Christ [22].[52] The inscription below Christ warns the viewer: *Cave cave d[omin]us videt* ('Beware, beware, the Lord sees'). The central circle is often interpreted as some sort of 'divine eye'. At the corners of the table, four smaller circles contain representations of the events predicted to happen at the end of the world, often referred to as the four 'Last Things': Death, the Last Judgement, Hell and Heavenly Glory.

In this representation it is not pride but anger (*ira*) that takes pride of place, just below the tomb of the risen Christ, on the largest section of the circle.[53] For an object that is a veritable compendium of theological meaning, the scenes showing the seven sins seem remarkably mundane.

This might say something about its original function. By the 1560s the extraordinary object was in the possession of the famously pious King Philip II of Spain, who hung it on the wall in his private quarters in the Escorial, outside Madrid, but before that it was very likely to have been an actual tabletop.[54] If we again turn to the *ira* panel, it becomes clear how sin might be a useful subject for a table. The scene depicts a violent brawl outside an inn, with pieces of furniture, including a table, being thrown around. The section showing gluttony (*gula*) again features a table, this time laden with food and drink, while two men gorge and a child attempts to do the same. The *Table of the Seven Deadly Sins* seems to connect the high with the low, and is a stark reminder of humankind's propensity to sin. How this object was practically used remains uncertain, but it has an immersive quality that is highly evocative.

Another object with similar attributes can be found in the British Museum. It is a tankard embellished with personifications of each of the seven sins on small amber panels [20]. If it was not made for Queen Christina of Sweden herself, then it certainly belonged to someone associated with the Swedish Royal House of Vasa, and was probably the creation of a craftsman from Königsberg in East Prussia.[55] The most appropriate of its seven personifications is gluttony, a corpulent woman holding a small chicken and fluted wine cup accompanied by a wild boar [21]. Swedish courtiers imbibing large quantities of wine and beer from

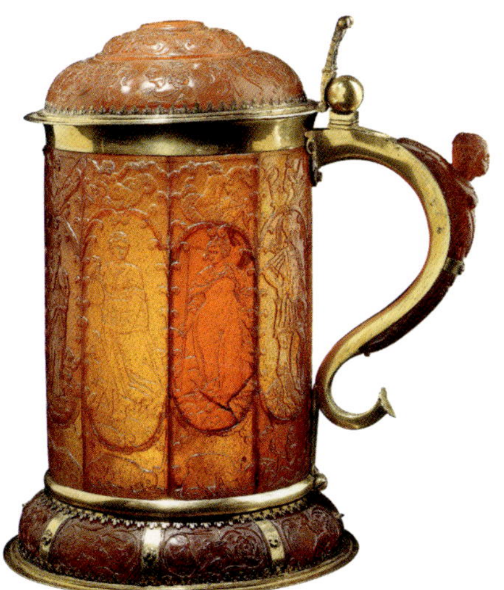

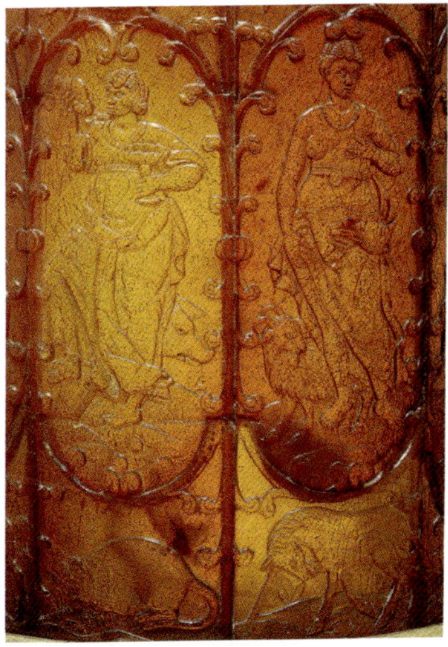

**20, 21** (detail) Anonymous craftsman from Königsberg (East Prussia), *Cylindrical Tankard with Personifications of the Seven Sins*, 1640–60. Silver, ivory, enamel, amber, 20.5 × 14 cm. The British Museum, London

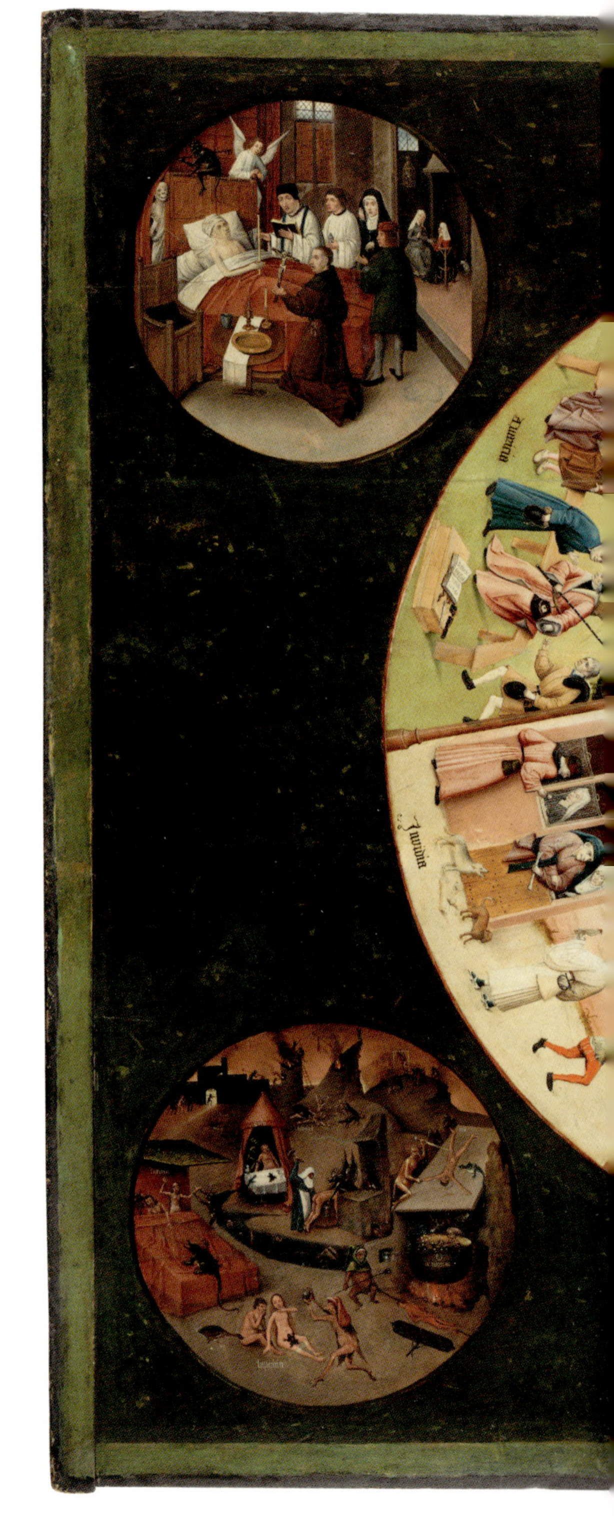

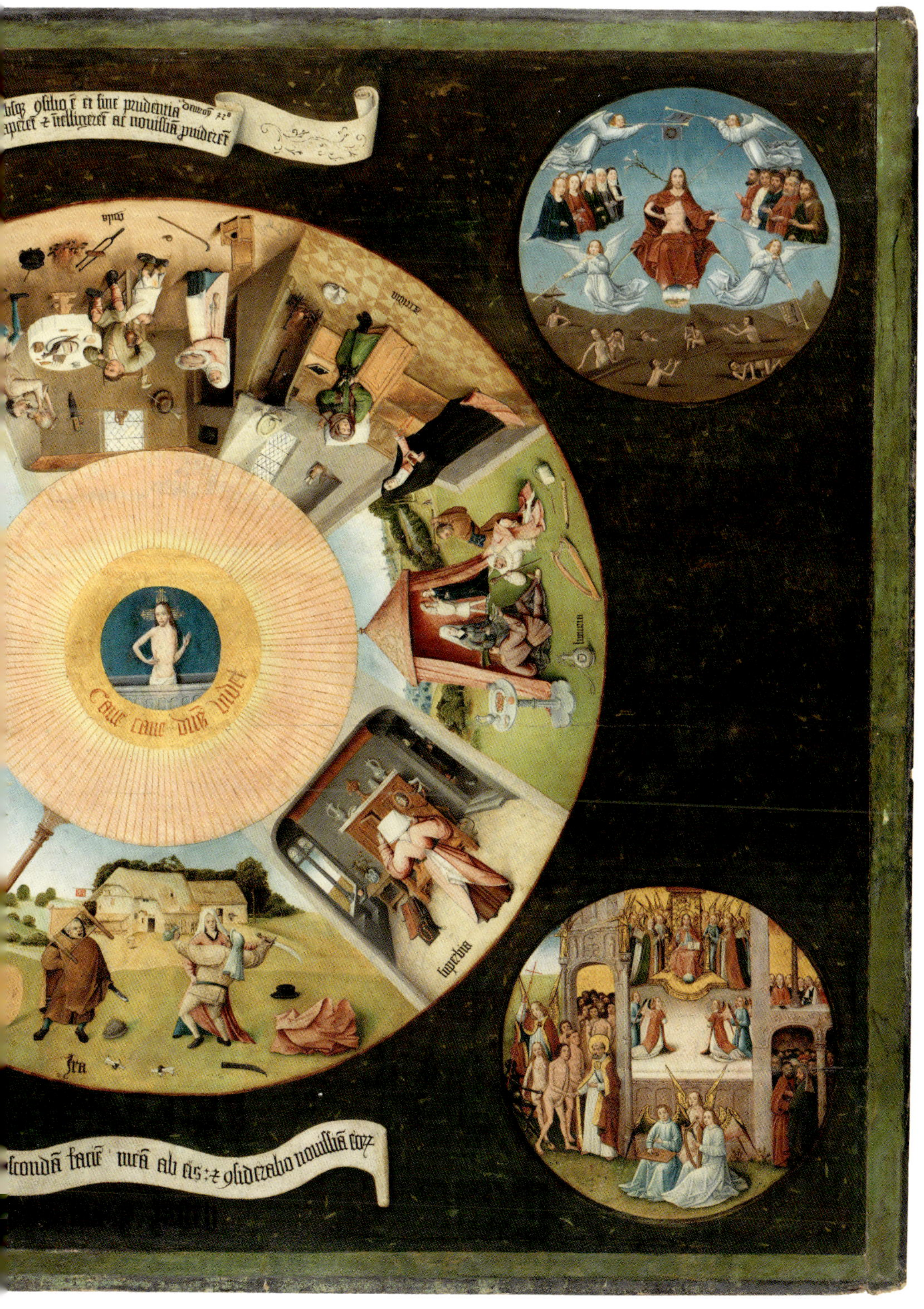


**22** Hieronymus Bosch (or workshop?) (1450–1516), *Table of the Seven Deadly Sins*, 1505–10. Oil on poplar, 119.5 × 139.5 cm. Museo Nacional del Prado, Madrid

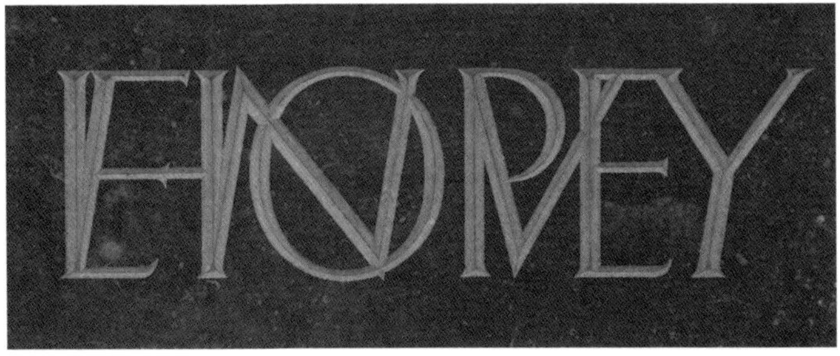

**23** Bruce Nauman (born 1941), *Hope/Envy* from *Seven Virtues/Seven Vices*, 1983–4. Limestone, in seven parts, 60.3 × 120 × 6 cm. The Museum of Modern Art, New York

the tankard would have been confronted with their sins every time they took a swig. Below the personification of gluttony we see an overfed cat, itself gluttonous – quite literally a 'fat cat'![56]

The seven sins proved a fertile artistic subject for many centuries to come. In Bruce Nauman's much later *Seven Virtues/Seven Vices* each of the seven limestone slabs bears the name of one of the seven sins superimposed on its accompanying virtue: prudence and pride, fortitude and anger (wrath), faith and lust, hope and envy, charity and sloth, temperance and gluttony, justice and avarice (greed) [23]. The result – an entangled, illegible mess of words – is yet another imaginative play on sin's ambiguities. It makes one wonder about the fluid boundaries between each sin and each virtue. Interestingly, Nauman's stone slabs also recall the ten divine commandments written on stone tablets, which the prophet Moses gave to the Jewish people.

The seven sins rarely come individually, in life or in painting, but often serve as the ingredients for a 'sinful cocktail'. Painters such as Jan Steen and William Hogarth knew exactly how to create the perfect mix. 'Een huishouden van Jan Steen' ('a Jan Steen household') is a common Dutch expression for a chaotic and unruly home.[57] In 1718–21 Steen's first biographer, Arnold Houbraken, equated the painter with his oeuvre: 'his paintings are like his lifestyle, and his lifestyle like his paintings.'[58] The trope that a work of art is a reflection of the maker's personality is an old one, and sometimes artists even celebrated their unruly reputations.[59] Houbraken's biography of Steen is filled with anecdotal debauchery and jokes, but in his case it seems at least partially inspired by the content of his pictures.

Steen's painting *The Effects of Intemperance* [24] shows sin and temptation everywhere in a household where the natural order has been overturned, and the children and servants have taken over. The pig about to devour a rose thrown in front of it refers to a Dutch saying akin to 'casting pearls before swine'. The mother of the household has fallen into an intoxicated slumber. Her pipe is about to drop from her right hand, and the wine she was drinking is now being offered to a domesticated parrot by the older daughter. Three younger children feed a pie to their pet cat [25]. The obvious sins theatrically on display are gluttony and sloth, with food and drink scattered all over the picture's foreground. One of the possible moral lessons to be taken from this scene is that bad behaviour inspires worse behaviour: the parrot is emblematic of imitation, and one of the youngest children is already transgressing in front of our eyes, as he picks his mother's pocket.[60] In fact, here a lesser sin seems to inspire a worse one. Steen painted the play of cause and effect: the basket above the woman's head contains the crutch and the clapper that are synonymous with the beggar, a warning of what could be in store.[61] Although Steen seems here to have secularised sin, the church looming in the distance serves as a reminder of a better path.

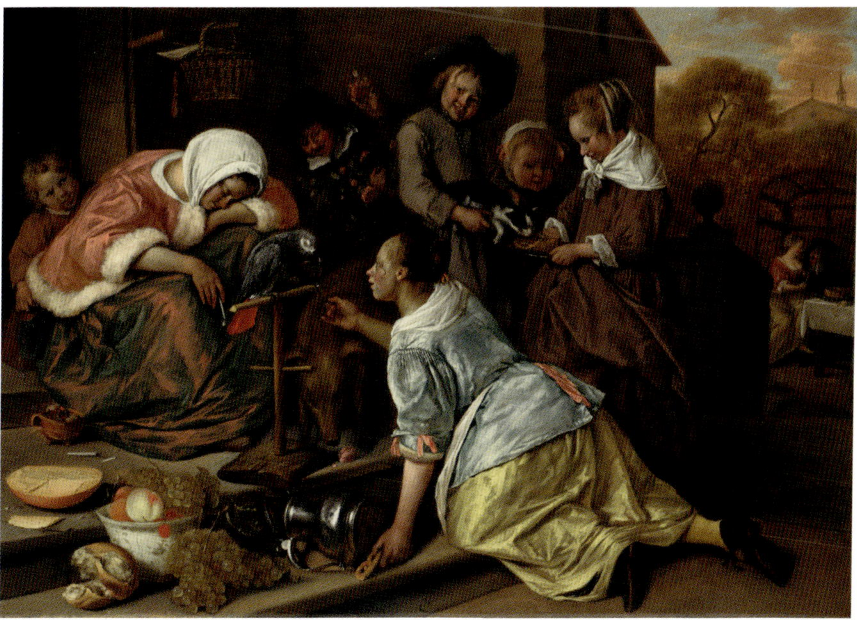

**24, 25** (detail, overleaf) Jan Steen (1626–1679), *The Effects of Intemperance*, about 1663–5. Oil on wood, 76 × 106.5 cm. The National Gallery, London

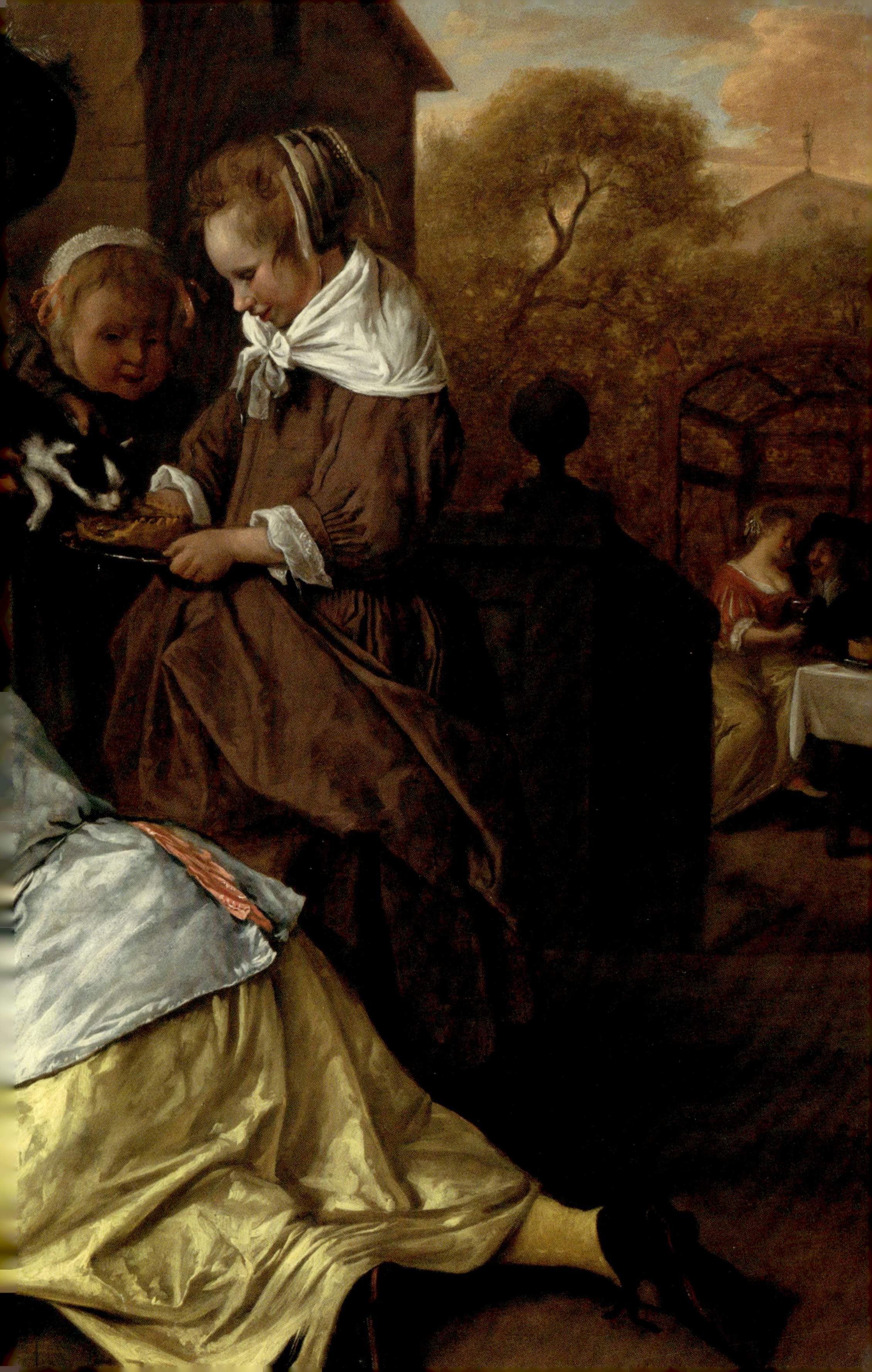

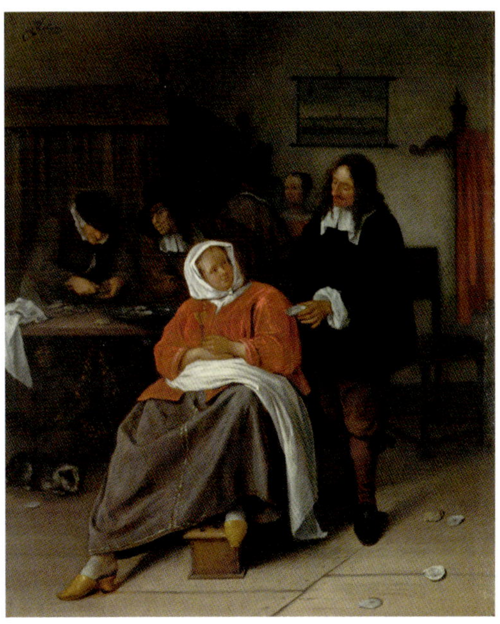

**26** Jan Steen (1626–1679), *An Interior with a Man offering an Oyster to a Woman*, probably 1660–5. Oil on oak, 38.1 × 31.5 cm. The National Gallery, London

Below the church, Steen reserved the right-hand background for something more lustful, although probably also induced by alcohol. A man is seduced by a young woman [25]. She sits on his lap drinking wine as she rubs her foot against the man's, bringing her cleavage close to his face. Maybe this is another reference to these children's futures? The woman may be a prostitute. The painter often explored prostitution in his work, such as the brothel scene in the euphemistically titled *An Interior with a Man offering an Oyster to a Woman* [26]. The symbolism in such salacious scenes is thinly veiled. Although Steen was Catholic, decorum prohibited the largely Calvinist Dutch (part of the Protestant Christian Church) to paint anything as risqué as Bronzino's *Allegory*.[62] The oysters in Steen's *Interior* are a symbol of lust, an obvious aphrodisiac and a reference to female sexuality.

William Hogarth could be considered eighteenth-century England's heir to Steen's didactic satires of seventeenth-century Holland.[63] Indeed, Hogarth's oeuvre has been characterised as a means 'to teach the people the rewards of virtue and the wages of sin'.[64] Hogarth even painted a personification of sin in an unfinished oil sketch, *Satan, Sin and Death* (Tate, London).[65] If Hogarth's paintings are lessons, there is a lot to be learned from his *Marriage A-la-Mode* series. The second scene in particular, *The Tête à Tête*, is a masterclass in sinful behaviour [28]. The set of six pictures tell the scandalous story of a disastrous marriage of convenience between a wasteful aristocrat's son and the daughter of a social climber.[66] Like Bosch's tabletop, *Marriage A-la-Mode* contains enough sins to fill this book. The series was partly inspired by a play of the same name by the great English dramatist John Dryden, which was first performed in 1672.[67] The story commences with *The Marriage Settlement* [27], depicting the marriage negotiations between the father of the groom, the 'Earl of Squander', and the father of the bride, while the soon-to-be newlyweds sit by indifferently. After that comes *The Tête à Tête*, followed by *The Inspection* [29], in which the young lord visits a doctor's surgery seeking a cure for syphilis, which all the other figures in the scene also seem to suffer from. Thinking back to interpretations of Bronzino's picture, the infectious disease seems to be a recurring theme. *The Toilette* [30] takes the viewer to the female protagonist's boudoir – she is now a countess – as she is getting ready for the day in the company of guests, a fashionable ritual that London's elite adopted from the French court. *The Bagnio* [31] meanwhile, transports us to the countess's nocturnal illicit encounter, the dire consequences of which are recorded in the last painting of the series, *The Lady's Death* [32]. Under Hogarth's societal microscope, sins escalate at a rapid pace.

To fully understand Hogarth's sinful series, we need to take a closer look at *The Tête à Tête*. The 'couple of convenience' sprawl slothfully in their Palladian London townhouse. They both seem exhausted and already fed up with each other. Even the servant in the background is yawning next to a table set up for card games. The wife has tea for one, an indication of the separate life she leads from her husband. The husband, meanwhile, does not even bother to fully hide his mistress's cap in his pocket, at which the dog sniffs [33]. A large black spot denoting syphilis is clearly visible on his neck, and the portrait bust on the mantelpiece with its patched-up nose is another more veiled reference to the same venereal disease.[68] The wife's satisfied expression hints at her part in more adultery. The steward of the household rolls his eyes as he exits with a stack of unpaid bills. The amount of detail

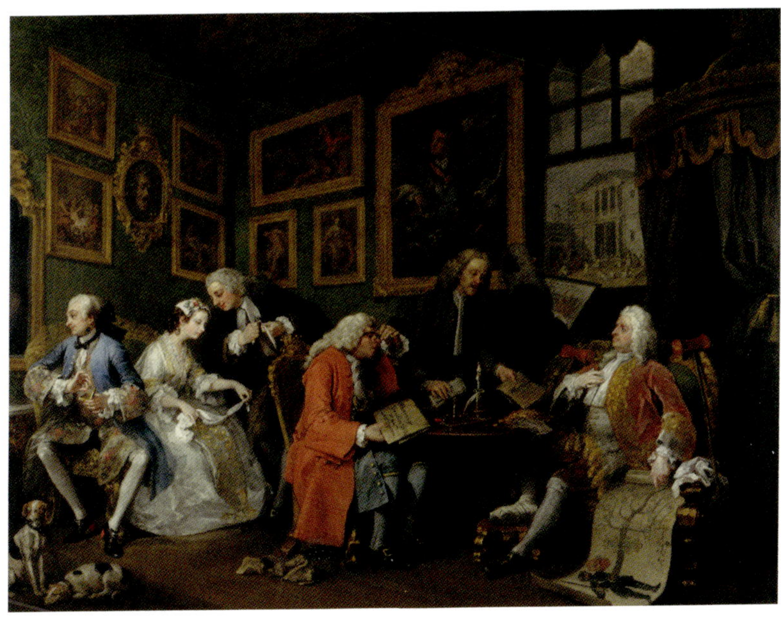

**27** William Hogarth (1697–1764), *Marriage A-la-Mode: 1, The Marriage Settlement,* about 1743. Oil on canvas, 69.9 × 90.8 cm. The National Gallery, London

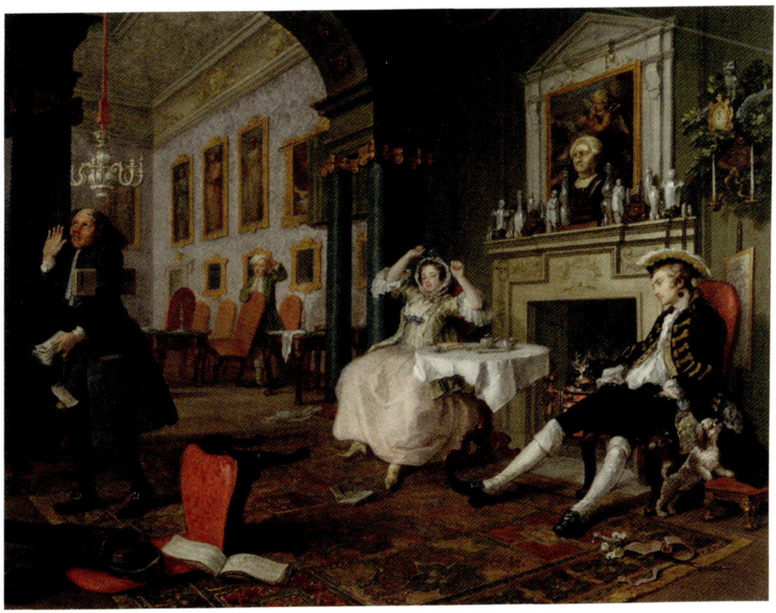

**28, 33** (detail pp. 50–1) William Hogarth (1697–1764), *Marriage A-la-Mode: 2, The Tête à Tête*, about 1743. Oil on canvas, 69.9 × 90.8 cm. The National Gallery, London

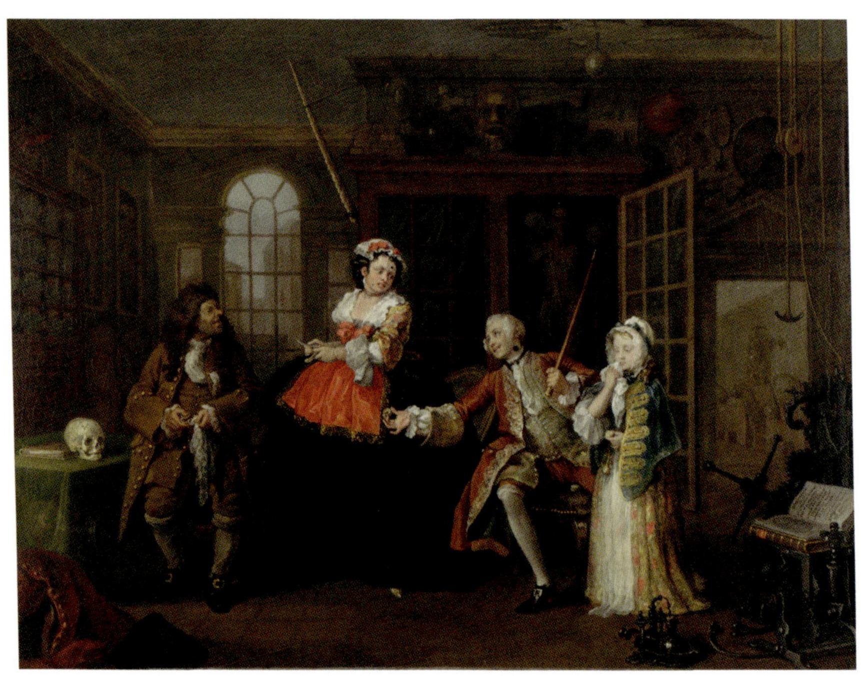

**29** William Hogarth (1697–1764), *Marriage A-la-Mode: 3, The Inspection*, about 1743. Oil on canvas, 69.9 × 90.8 cm. The National Gallery, London

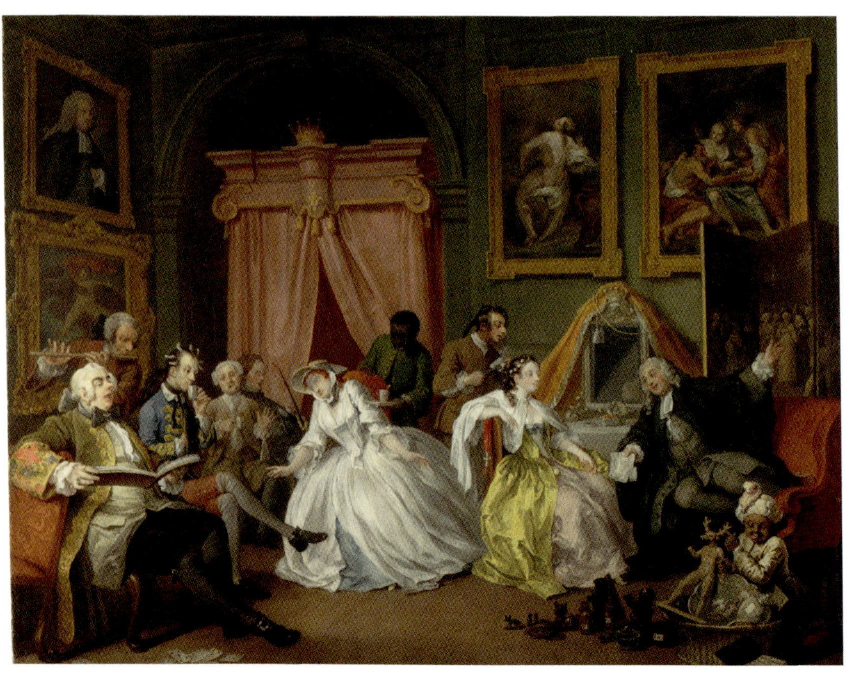

**30** William Hogarth (1697–1764), *Marriage A-la-Mode: 4, The Toilette*, about 1743. Oil on canvas, 70.5 × 90.8 cm, The National Gallery, London

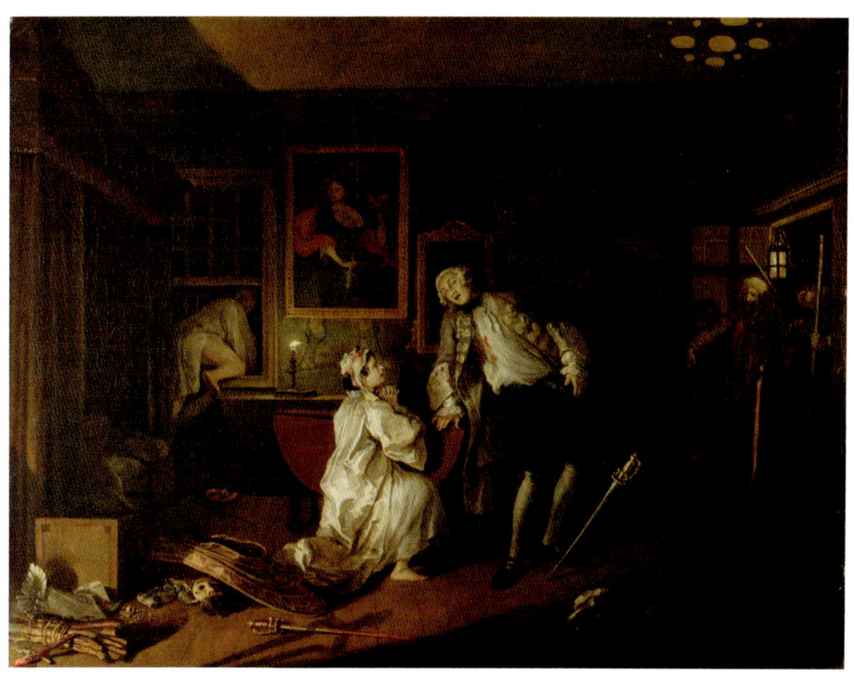

**31** William Hogarth (1697–1764), *Marriage A-la-Mode: 5, The Bagnio*, about 1743. Oil on canvas, 70.5 × 90.8 cm. The National Gallery, London

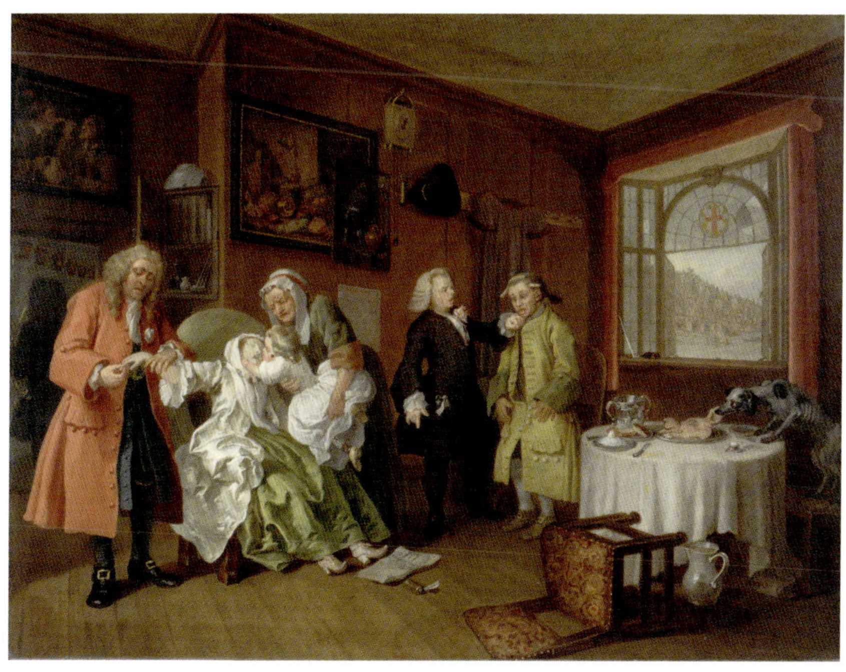

**32** William Hogarth (1697–1764), *Marriage A-la-Mode: 6, The Lady's Death*, about 1743. Oil on canvas, 69.9 × 90.8 cm. The National Gallery, London

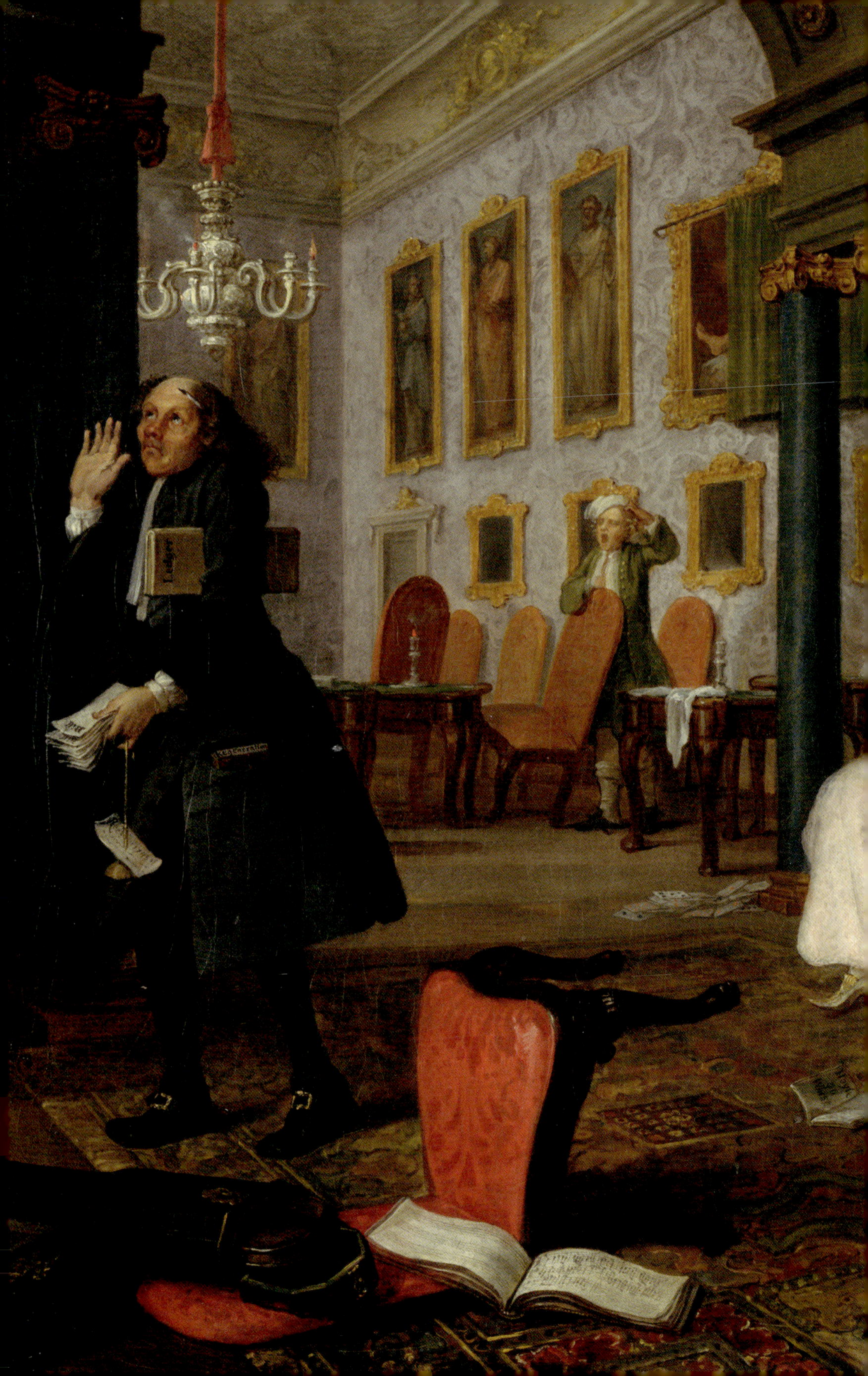

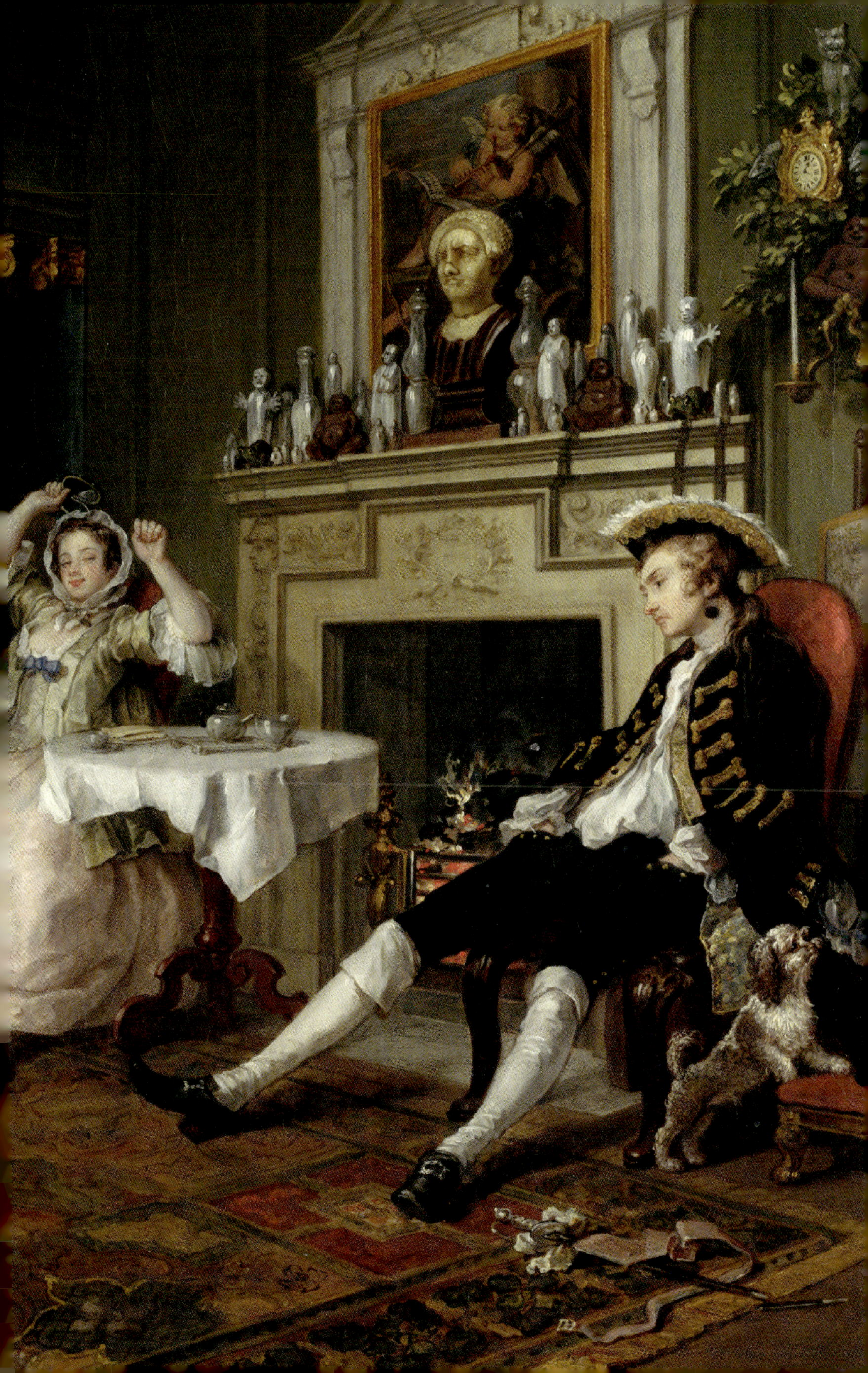

in *The Tête à Tête* is astounding. Hogarth loved painting real or imagined pictures within his pictures. In the backroom we see one of them, partly covered by a curtain [33]. Only a foot sticks out, suggesting its subject could be a recumbent Venus. Like the owner of Bronzino's *Allegory*, Monsieur Beaucousin, his lordship has covered his improper picture. Perhaps some of Cranach's Venuses received similar treatment? To the left of the curtained picture in Hogarth's scene of sin are four pictures showing full-length saints. The juxtaposition between saints and sensuality highlights the moral hypocrisy that is rife in the series.

'Paintings within paintings' say a lot in Hogarth, something he might have picked up from seventeenth-century Dutch masters. The male counterpart in the countess's affair, for instance, is 'revealed' by the pictures above their heads in *The Toilette*. They are existing pictures, Correggio's *Jupiter and Io* and *Lot and his Daughters*, two scenes of seduction, one from classical antiquity and the other from the Old Testament. The man making himself comfortable next to her ladyship is the lawyer Silvertongue, the same man already whispering in her ear in *The Marriage Settlement* – clearly he ended up getting more than just her ear. Steen and Hogarth painted deliciously sinful scenes.

Some pictures in the National Gallery's collection have a more specific sinful focus. Going back to Botticelli's drawing for Dante's *Comedy*, it seems that on Saint Augustine's authority many people consider pride (or *superbia*) the supreme sin, the one which makes humans forget their relative importance in comparison with God, seeking to usurp his position. Being 'as God' is exactly what is on the minds of the multitude depicted in Leandro Bassano's *Tower of Babel* [34]. The building of the Tower of Babel is a classic example of the sin of pride. The episode takes us back to the Book of Genesis once more, this time after the episode of the Flood, in which God had killed off all the sinful people, saving only Noah's virtuous family to start the world afresh. Here, the story's protagonist, Nimrod, a descendant of Noah, appears rather lavishly dressed in the picture's middle ground, seemingly instructing the builders. Their enterprise is summarised in Genesis 11: 4: 'Come, let us build ourselves a city, and a tower with its top in the heavens, and let us make a name for ourselves; otherwise we shall be scattered abroad upon the face of the whole earth.'

It is not difficult to explain why building a tower 'with its top in the heavens' to 'make a name' for oneself might be considered prideful.

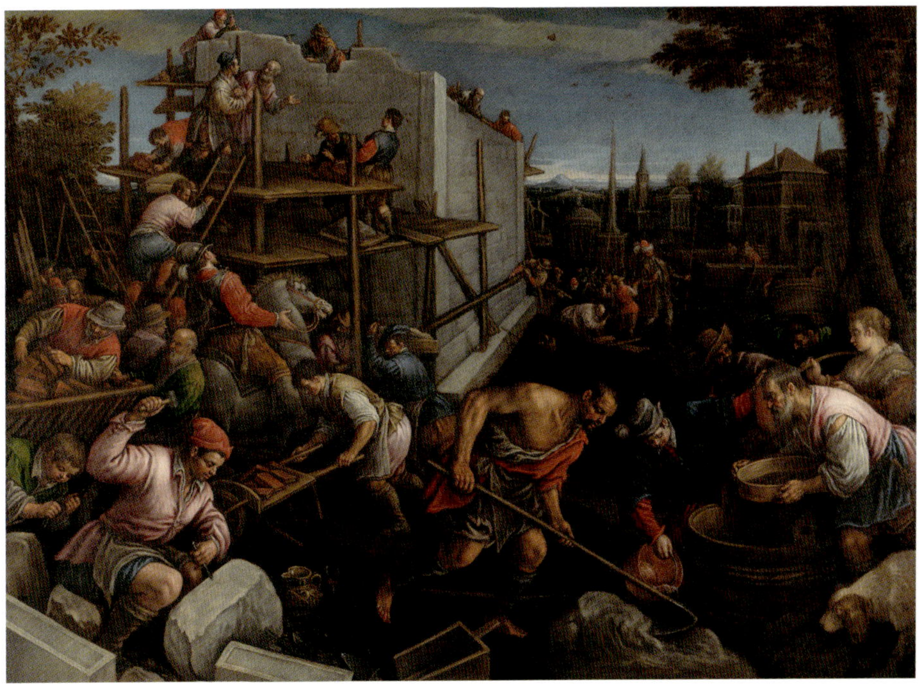

**34** Leandro Bassano (1557–1622), *The Tower of Babel*, about 1600. Oil on canvas, 137.1 × 189.2 cm. The National Gallery, London

God's punishment was highly effective. He took the builders and scattered them all over the earth, where they had always been in one place together. Furthermore, he made them speak different languages so that they wouldn't be able to communicate and plot further sacrilegious acts. The episode shows how the story of sin affects us all. We would all speak the same language and be living harmoniously in the Garden of Eden – if it had not been for our pride…

Another example of a picture focusing on a specific sin is Jean-Honoré Fragonard's *Psyche showing her Sisters her Gifts from Cupid* [35]. Unlike Bassano's story from the Old Testament, this picture depicts an episode from classical literature, the *Metamorphoses* (sometimes called *The Golden Ass*) by the Roman writer Apuleius. The seven sins are as abundant in the classics as they are in the Bible. Apuleius recounts how Psyche's siblings are looking for their lost sister. When they find her, Psyche invites them into her house:

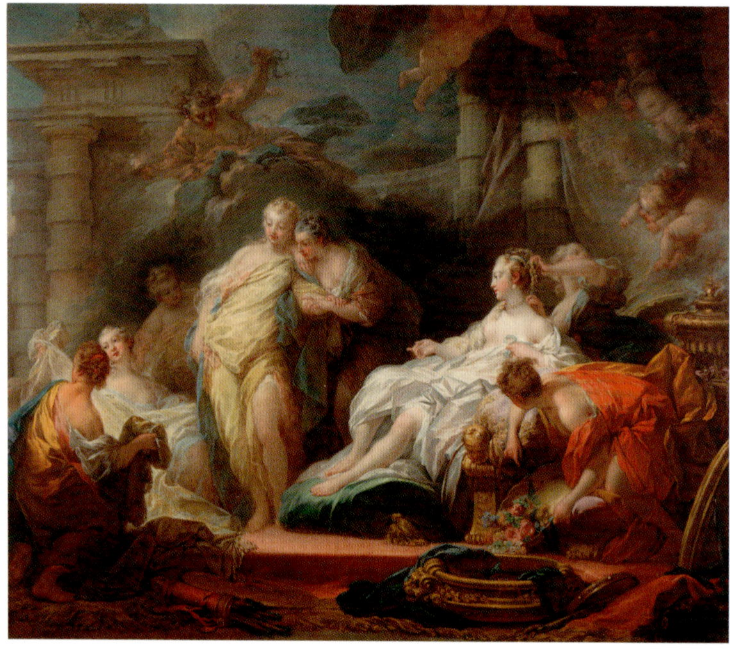

**35** Jean-Honoré Fragonard (1732–1806), *Psyche showing her Sisters her Gifts from Cupid*, 1753. Oil on canvas, 168.3 × 192.4 cm. The National Gallery, London

> 'But come under our roof,' Psyche said, 'enter our home in happiness, and refresh your troubled souls together with your Psyche.' [ … ] She refreshed them luxuriously with a beautiful bath and the delicacies of her unearthly table; with the result that, glutted with the abundant plenty of this truly heavenly wealth, they began to nourish envy deep in their hearts.[69]

Envy, or jealousy, is the sin that dominates Apuleius' episode from the love story between Psyche and Cupid. Psyche's sisters are not happy that Cupid has showered their sister with opulent gifts. Quite the contrary. When they return home '... those worthy sisters were consumed with the gall of swelling Envy and complained loud and long to each other'.[70] Fragonard painted Psyche's sisters examining her new-found riches as her nymphs tend to her. A Medusa-like personification of Envy hurls itself from the clouds above Psyche's sisters, as if animating their jealousy [36]. Envy clutches snakes with its left hand. At this point, the association between snakes and sin should no longer surprise the reader. The large canvas was presented to a patron who was used to the finer things in life, the French King Louis XV at Versailles in 1753.[71] We can only speculate how Louis must have interpreted the picture's subject.

Even in a picture like Fragonard's, which clearly has envy at the heart of its subject, the presence of other sins is palpable. Was Psyche after all not moved by pride? Perhaps more specific in subject is a picture titled *Two Tax-Gatherers*, from the workshop of Marinus van Reymerswale [37]. This grotesque image seems to be about greed, and a popular Dutch rhyme links the sin of greed with other money-related occupations as the Devil's work:

> A usurer,
> A miller,
> A money-changer,
> And a tax-collector,
> Are Lucifer's Four Evangelists.[72]

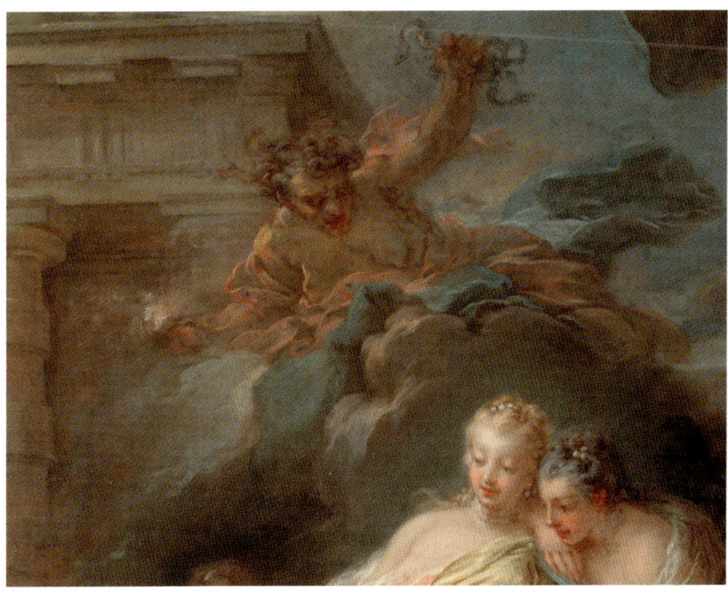

**36** Detail from *Psyche showing her Sisters her Gifts from Cupid*

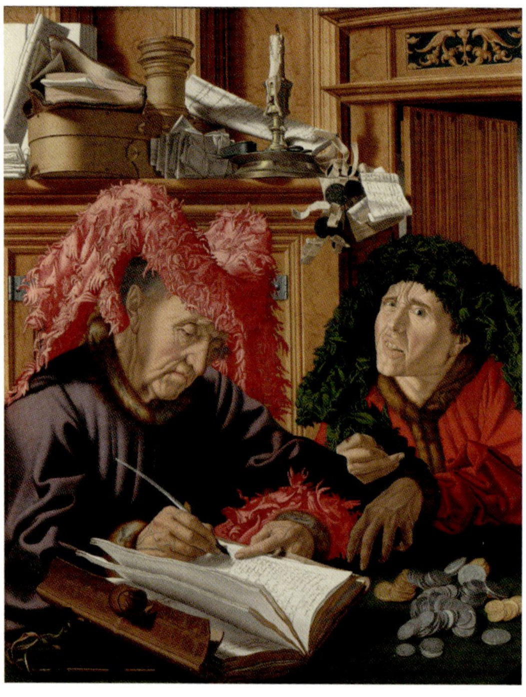

**37** Workshop of Marinus van Reymerswale (active 1533–1545), *Two Tax-Gatherers*, probably 1540s. Oil on oak, 92 × 74.6 cm. The National Gallery, London

One could imagine David Teniers the Younger's *The Rich Man being led to Hell* as depicting the fate of the *Two Tax-Gatherers* and a vindication of the foreboding rhyme [38]. The parable stems from the Gospel of Luke (16: 19–31), which tells the story of how the affluent man, acting out of greed, ignored the beggar Lazarus lying at his gate. The look of fear in the man's eyes speak volumes, as fantastical demons drag him down to the depths of hell.

## THE REDEEMER

From what we have seen in our story so far, it appears that humanity sins relentlessly. Luckily for humankind this is only part of the story. There is the possibility of redemption; to atone and make amends for past wrongdoing, the option of salvation. And in the biblical narrative, specifically that told in the New Testament, there is one ultimate

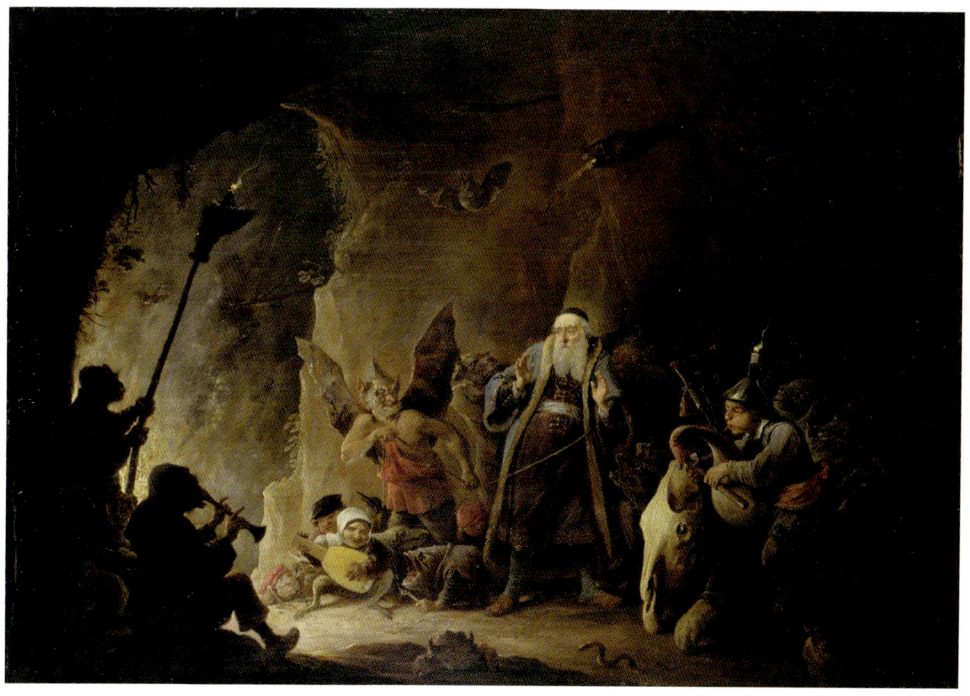

**38** David Teniers the Younger (1610–1690), *The Rich Man being led to Hell*, about 1647. Oil on oak, 48 × 69 cm. The National Gallery, London

redeemer, put on Earth by God to save Adam and Eve's offspring from their sins and restore their relationship with their creator. We have of course encountered the saviour figure a couple of times already, for instance in Gossaert's small *Virgin and Child* [see 9], where Christ is heralded as the one who will save us from our sins. But Gossaert's picture is just one of the many eloquent examples in the National Gallery's collection that speak to this theme.[73] Another ingenious example is a fifteenth-century panel of *The Presentation in the Temple* by the so-called Master of the Life of the Virgin [39]. The panel was commissioned as part of an altarpiece for the church of Saint Ursula in Cologne. It is by no means a picture with a simple message.

The moment of the presentation of Christ to the aged priest Simeon (who recognised the infant's divinity) is closely associated with Christ's circumcision in many visual representations, which can be read symbolically as the first time that Jesus would shed his blood for humankind's salvation before his crucifixion. The fact that all of this takes place beside an altar would have strong Eucharistic connotations for Christian worshippers, reminding them of the Mass. The altar is the place where bread and wine are consecrated and consumed as Christ's body and blood during the act of worship commemorating his death on behalf of his followers. The altarpiece within the picture completes the narrative of Christ's triumph over sin by shedding his own blood [40]. 'A work of art within a work of art' is used here, just as we saw the three reliefs in Botticelli's drawing for *Purgatorio* [see 1]. The three scenes that make up the triptych within the painting are Cain slaying Abel (Adam and Eve's first sons); the attempted sacrifice of Isaac by his father Abraham; and the drunkenness of Noah. Each of these Old Testament scenes prefigures Christ's death on the Cross. And more importantly, each scene speaks to the concept of sin: Cain killed Abel out of jealousy. Abel's offering was accepted by God when Cain's was not, after which God warned Cain that 'sin is lurking at the door' (Genesis 4: 7). Noah's naked drunkenness and subsequent discovery by his sons can easily be considered sinful, and is often compared to Adam and Eve's eating of the forbidden fruit and Cain's murder of Abel. The comparison

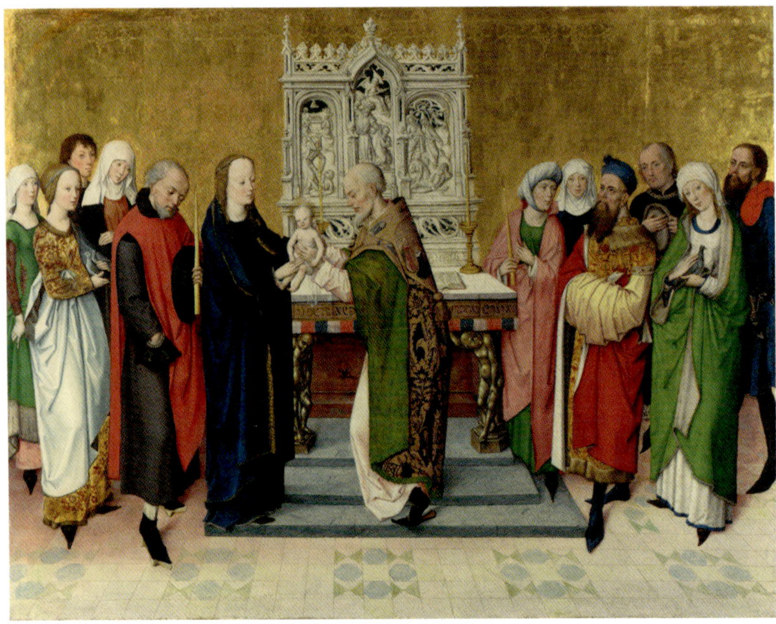

**39, 40** (opposite) Master of the Life of the Virgin (active second half of the 15th century), *The Presentation in the Temple*, probably about 1460–75. Oil on oak, 83.8 × 108.6 cm. The National Gallery, London

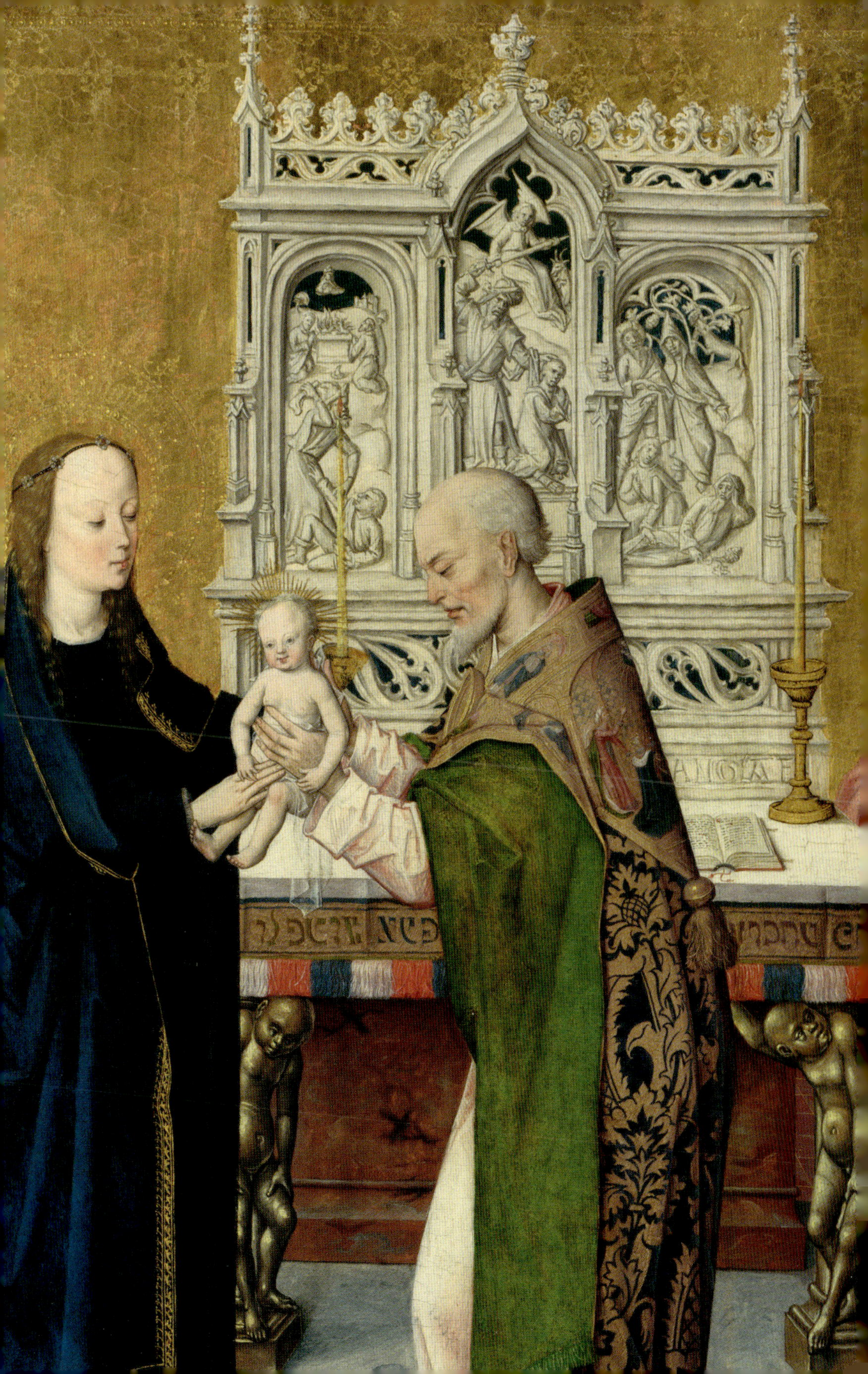

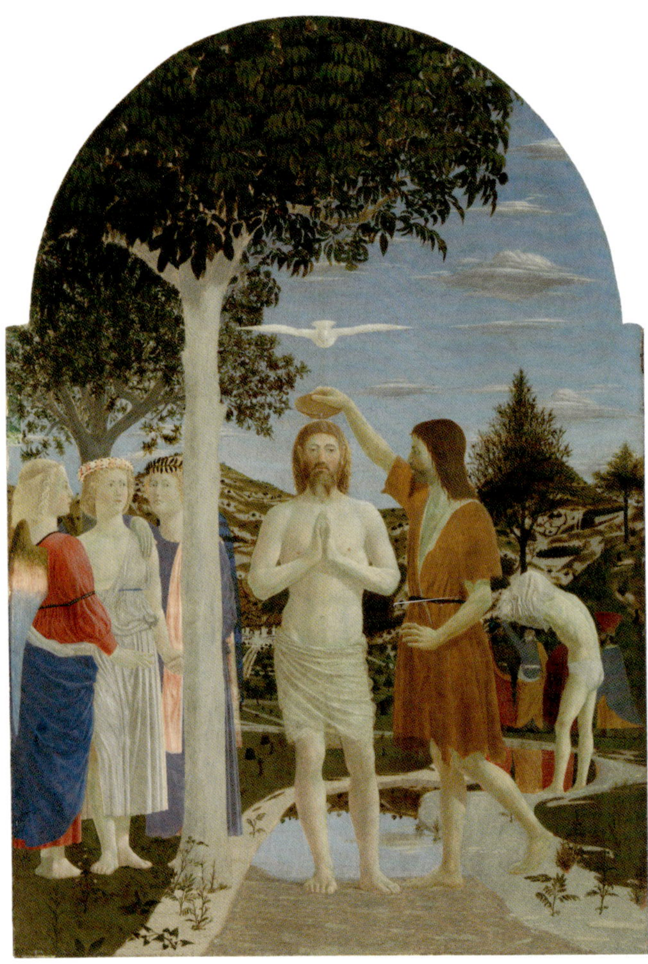

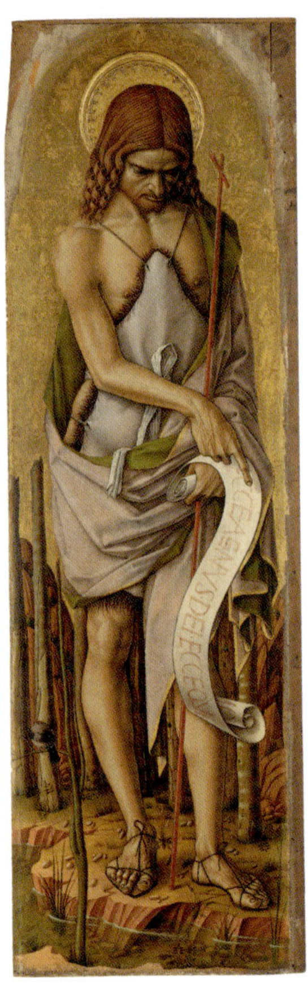

**41** Piero della Francesca (about 1415/20–1492), *The Baptism of Christ*, after 1437. Egg tempera on poplar, 167 × 116 cm. The National Gallery, London

**42** Carlo Crivelli (about 1430/5–about 1494), *Saint John the Baptist* from The Demidoff Altarpiece, 1476. Egg tempera on poplar, 138.5 × 40 cm. The National Gallery, London

highlights how sins were fundamental to the human world in the Garden of Eden, the world outside of Eden after the Expulsion, and the world after the Flood.[74] Abraham's attempted sacrifice of his son on a makeshift altar stands in a long tradition of sacrifice as a sin-offering, this one directly requested by God.[75] *The Presentation in the Temple* presents the ultimate sin-offering before the altar: Christ, staring directly at the viewer, in comparison with more 'common' offerings, the doves held by the flanking women.

In the story of Christ's life as recounted in the New Testament it is Saint John the Baptist who announces his cousin's role as the redeemer of humankind. It is in this role that Carlo Crivelli painted John on a multi-panelled altarpiece for the high altar of the church of San Domenico in Ascoli Piceno in the Italian Marche [42]. The saint points with his veined right hand at a Latin inscription on a scroll that reads: '*ECCE AGNUS DEI, ECCE QUI.*' The often-used wording is from John 1: 29: 'Here is the Lamb of God who takes away the sin of the world!' It is no coincidence that John looks down at a stream of flowing water in Crivelli's panel, since he was to baptise Christ in the river Jordan. Baptism is both an immersion for the removal of ritual uncleanness and a sacrament for absolution from sin.[76] There are few more evocative pictures of baptism than Piero della Francesca's *Baptism of Christ* [41]. But the idea that John baptised Christ proved controversial. If Christ was baptised, did this mean that he needed forgiveness for his own sins?[77] Theologians have interpreted his baptism as Christ making an outward sign that displays his humanity (for someone who was both human and divine) and humility. Humility, then, is a virtue, and not a sin, the opposite of pride.

Christians believe that redemption would ultimately manifest itself in Christ's crucifixion, where he died on behalf of humanity to pay the price, once and for all, for their sinfulness. This sacrifice was accepted and perfected through Christ being miraculously raised from the dead before being taken up into heaven. Ugolino di Nerio's small panel of *The Betrayal of Christ* shows the moment that led to his arrest and crucifixion [43]. The arrest was facilitated by Christ's disciple Judas, arguably the New Testament's worst sinner, who betrayed Christ by kissing him to confirm his identity. Raphael painted the aftermath of Judas' betrayal – Christ on the Cross – with arresting simplicity, symmetry and idealised beauty in another picture in the National

Gallery [44]. Christ's body stands out in stark contrast against the blue sky as two angels collect the blood that drips from the wounds in his hands and side. The chalices are reminiscent of those in which wine would be administered during Mass at the altar below. More blood drips from Christ's feet towards the base of the Cross. Here, one would usually expect to find Adam's skull. The place of Christ's death, Golgotha or Calvary, was widely believed to be the place of Adam's grave, and many painters placed this skull at the base of the Cross in their paintings. The blood flowing earthwards from Christ's feet visualises the world's redemption, and in this tradition Adam's skull would receive this redemptive blood first.[78] Raphael, however, did something else. He signed his picture at the base of the Cross between the flanking worshippers, saints Jerome and Mary Magdalene, '*RAPHAEL/ VRBIN/ AS/ P*' ('Raphael from Urbino painted this') [45]. Having already encountered Lucas Cranach's 'self-conscious' signature in *Adam and Eve* [see 6], such artistic feats are unsurprising. Raphael might have had his own salvation in mind, as the blood from Christ's wounds would theoretically reach his signature first as it moves towards the foot of the Cross.[79]

The unusual iconography of Simone dei Crocefissi's *Dream of the Virgin* explicitly connects Adam and Eve to the Crucifixion [46]. This early Bolognese painting might look bizarre, but it more or less distils

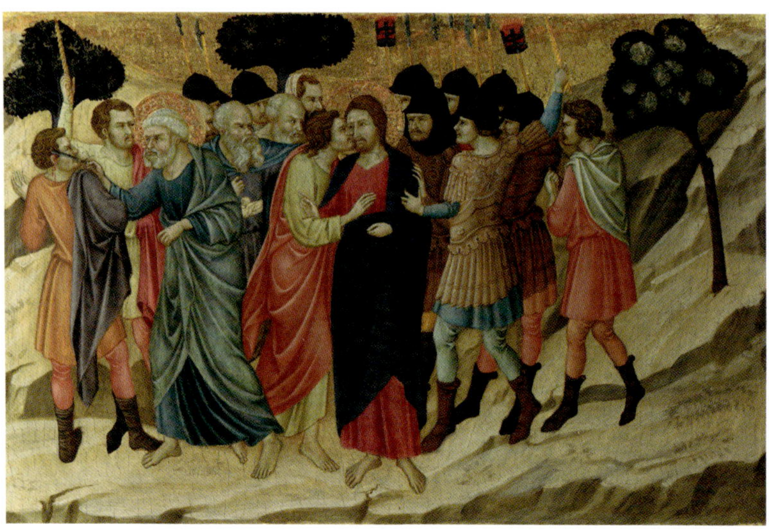

**43** Ugolino di Nerio (documented 1317–27; died possibly 1329), *The Betrayal of Christ*, possibly 1325–8. Egg tempera on poplar, 40.4 × 58.8 cm. The National Gallery, London

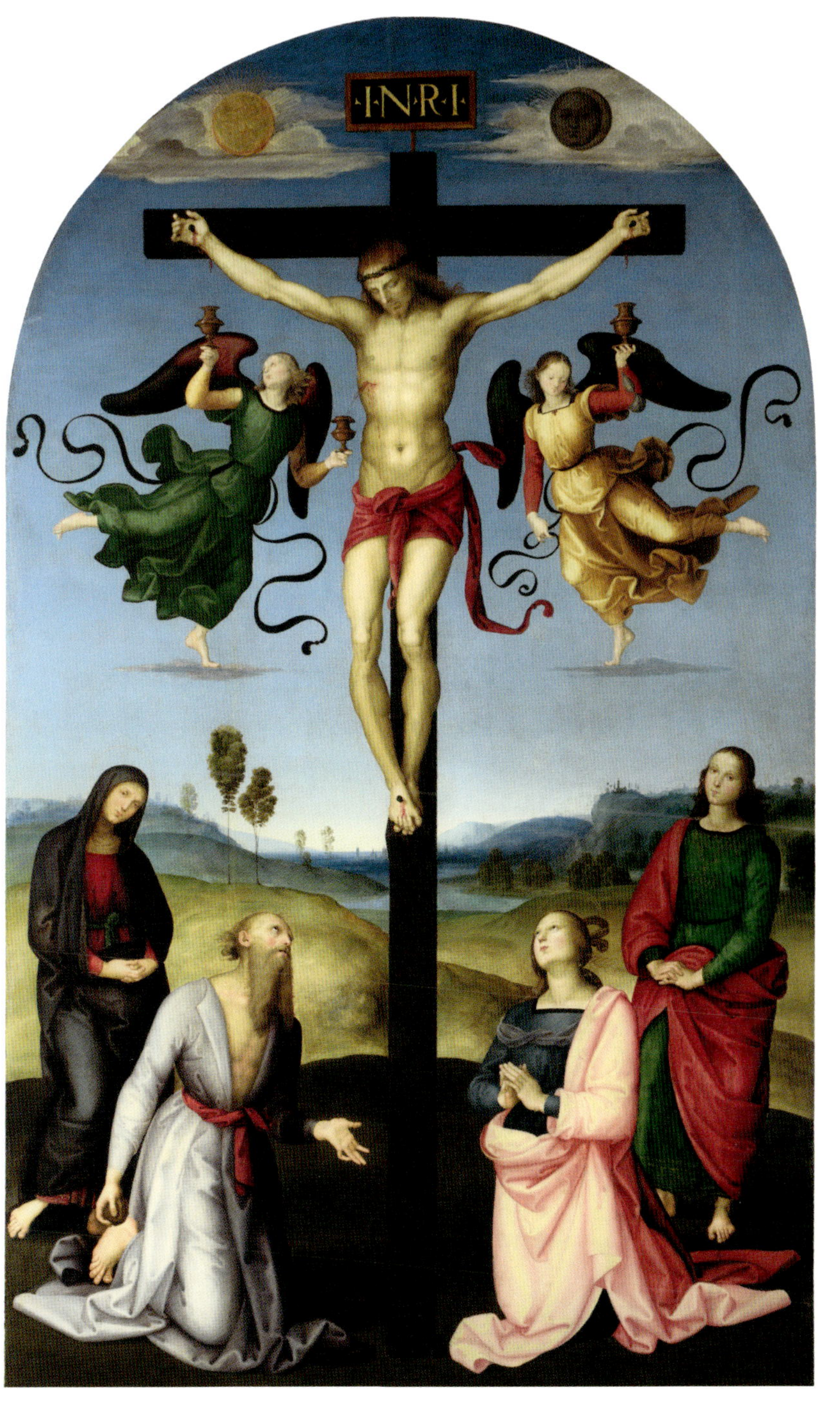


**44** Raphael (1483–1520), *The Crucified Christ with the Virgin Mary, Saints and Angels (The Mond Crucifixion)*, about 1502–3. Oil on poplar, 283.3 × 167.3 cm. The National Gallery, London

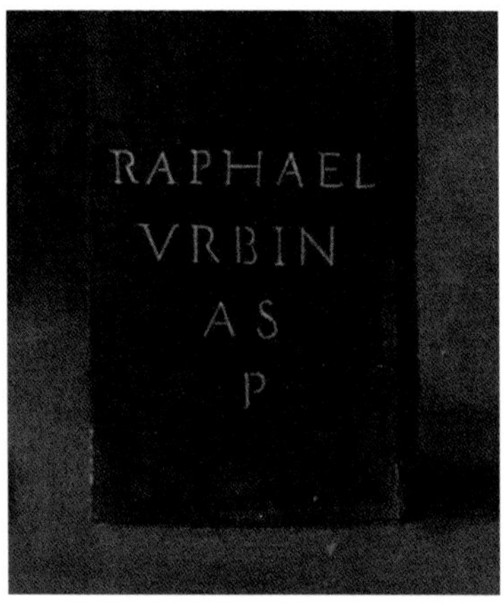


**45** Detail of the artist's signature from *The Mond Crucifixion*

the theological argument about sin and redemption in a single image. It was once part of a much larger multi-panelled altarpiece, probably the crowning panel or *cimasa*.[80] The crucified Christ appears to be growing out of the trunk of a vine rising from Mary's body as she lies asleep in bed.[81] The vine reminds us the Tree of Knowledge.[82] At the bottom of the tree/crucifix a hand miraculously appears from a small cloud and reaches down into a cave to grab Adam's outstretched left arm, with Eve just behind him. One could call this a 'redemptive hand'. Just as the blood flows down in many images of Christ's crucifixion, often reaching Adam's skull first – and on at least one occasion, Raphael's signature – here Adam and Eve seem very much alive, although much older than they appeared the last time we encountered them in Eden. The story hails from the so-called Gospel of Nicodemus which is not found in the Bible. According to this story, Christ was believed to have descended into hell to redeem the souls of those who, living before him, had not had the chance to be baptised into the Christian faith. We call this the 'Harrowing of Hell'.

Simone dei Crocefissi painted Adam and Eve as the first two waiting for Christ's posthumous salvation; they look on eagerly as the gates of hell are opened. Adam and Eve reappear in another painting in the National Gallery's collection, made by a Flemish painter for the Spanish Queen Isabella of Castile, once part of an ensemble of 47 small panels, Juan de Flandes's *Christ appearing to the Virgin with the Redeemed of*

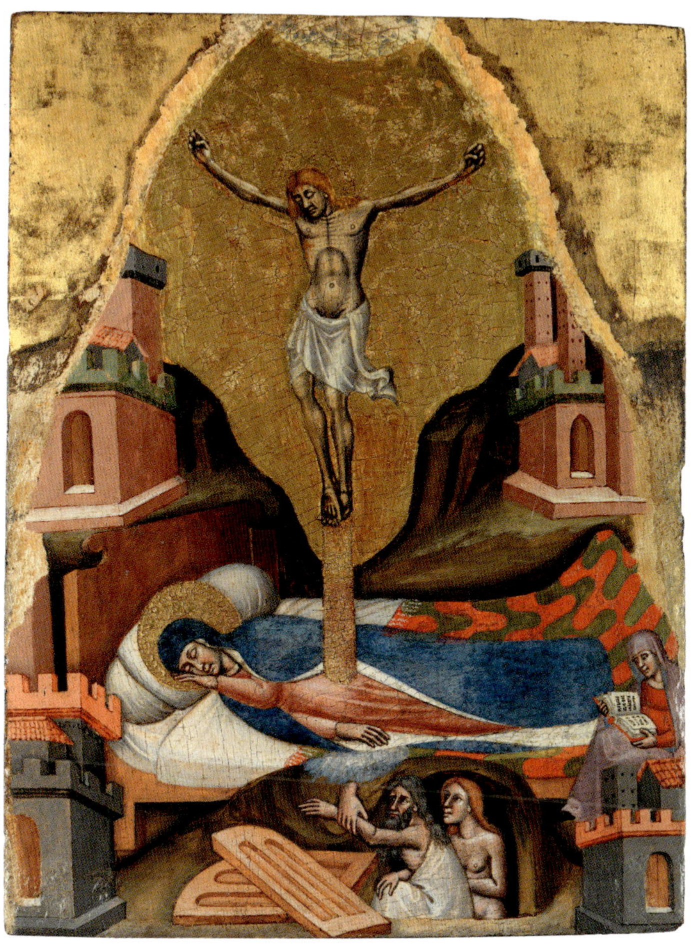

**46** Simone dei Crocefissi (active 1355–1399), *Dream of the Virgin*, about 1365–80. Egg tempera on wood, 56.6 × 42.5 cm. Society of Antiquaries of London on long term loan to the National Gallery

*the Old Testament* [47]. Adam and Eve are peering over Christ's right shoulder, and to his left we find John the Baptist, flanked by a couple likely to be Joachim and Anne, the Virgin Mary's parents.[83] It is another unusual scene that seems to take the narrative a stage further than in Simone dei Crocefissi's picture. Christ has returned from his journey to hell, and brought countless of the redeemed unbaptised to his mother who is not asleep but sitting in prayer by her bed.[84]

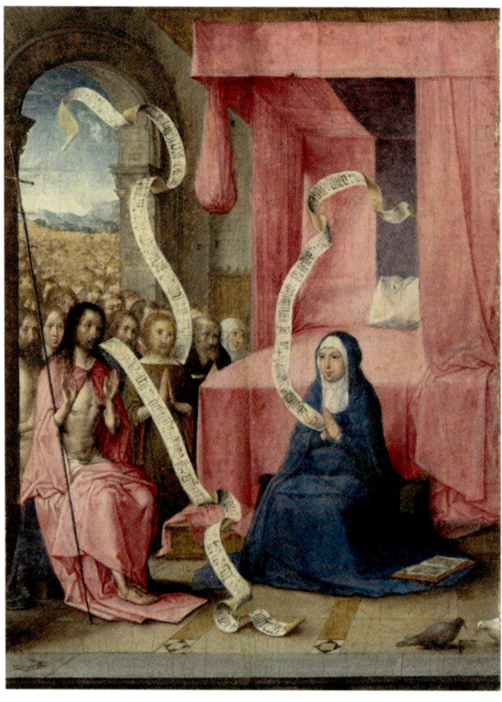

**47** Juan de Flandes (active from 1496; died 1519), *Christ appearing to the Virgin with the Redeemed of the Old Testament*, about 1499–1500. Oil on oak, 21.2 × 15.4 cm. The National Gallery, London

Christ's role in saving people from sin extended beyond his earthly life in the scenes we have explored so far. Annibale Carracci painted *Christ appearing to Saint Anthony Abbot during his Temptation* [48]. Saint Anthony's biography by the theologian Athanasius of Alexandria inspired many artists, not least among them the nineteenth-century French novelist Gustave Flaubert, who describes how the hermit is tempted by each of the seven deadly sins with gruesome abundance in *The Temptation of Saint Anthony*.[85] In Annibale's small picture these temptations take the shape of a variety of monstrous tormentors. There is a horned lion roaring and a devilish horned man with sharp claws and the wings of a bat. From the top of the cave a winged lizard with a human head appears. And from inside the darkest recesses of the cave emerges a Medusa-like creature with snakes entangled in its hair, wielding another snake as a weapon, its fangs ready to strike the frightened saint. The figure is not unlike the personification of *Envy*

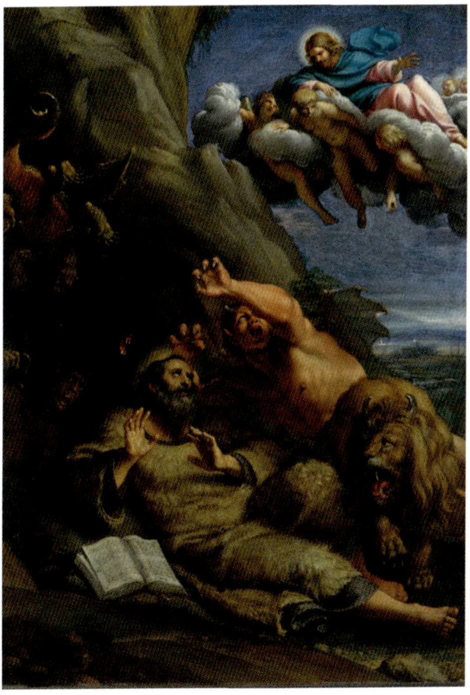

**48** Annibale Carracci (1560–1609), *Christ appearing to Saint Anthony Abbot*, about 1598. Oil on copper, 49.5 × 34.4 cm. The National Gallery, London

we saw in Fragonard's depiction of Psyche and her envious sisters [see 36]. In fact, another look at Hogarth's *Marriage Settlement* [27] reveals a framed 'portrait' of a similar serpent-haired figure above the bride-to-be. The association between snakes and sinful temptation is a constant in our story. Annibale's *Christ appearing to Saint Anthony Abbot* transports the viewer back to the third century when the saint experienced his temptations in the desert, and we also witness Christ there, eternally present to save. He appears on clouds carried by angels when Anthony needs him most. The saint's Christian faith saves him from sin, with the open book beside him reminding the viewer where to find redemption's source, namely in the Bible.

Are there episodes from Christ's life where he himself was tempted by sin, or in which he verged on sinning? One such scene comes to mind, painted by El Greco in his *Christ driving the Traders from the Temple* [49]. Christ appears angry, irate even (wrath being one of the

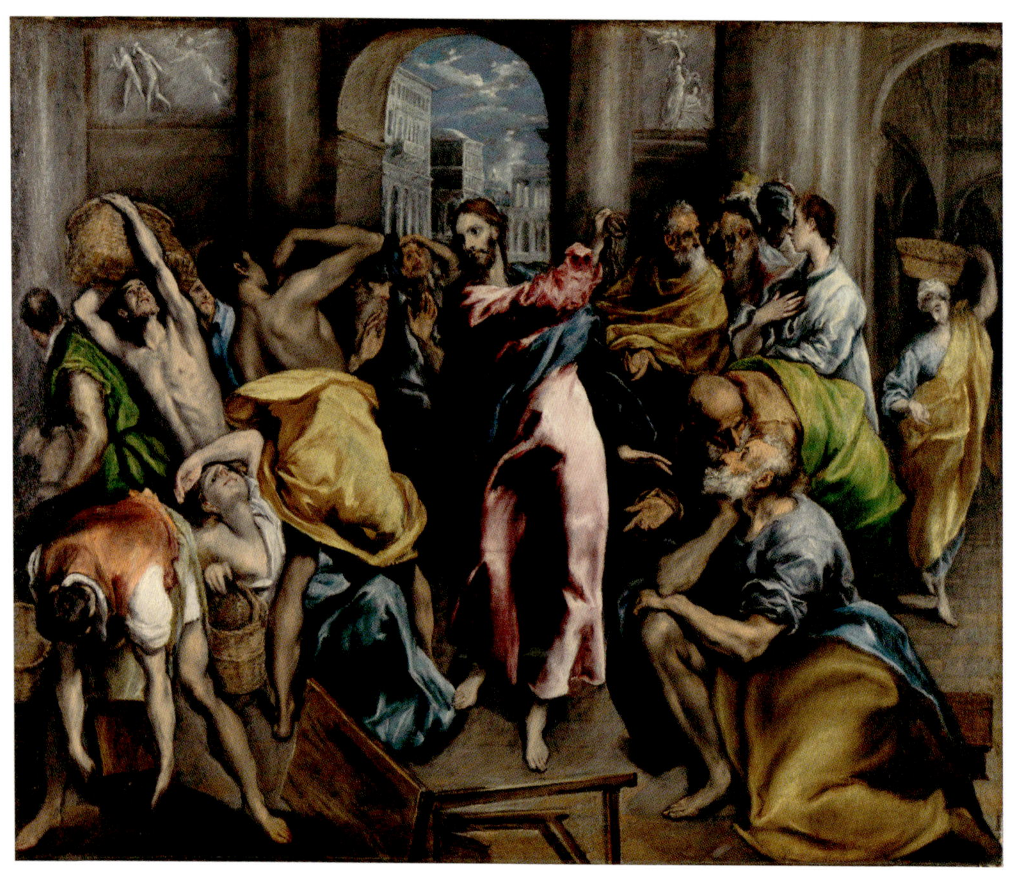

**49** El Greco (1541–1614), *Christ driving the Traders from the Temple*, about 1600. Oil on canvas, 106.3 × 129.7 cm. The National Gallery, London

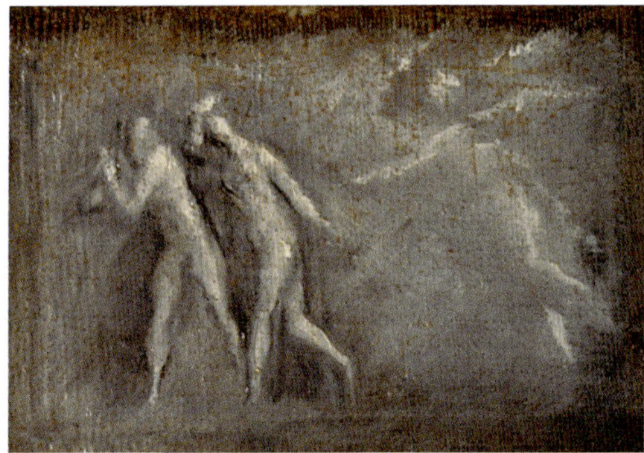
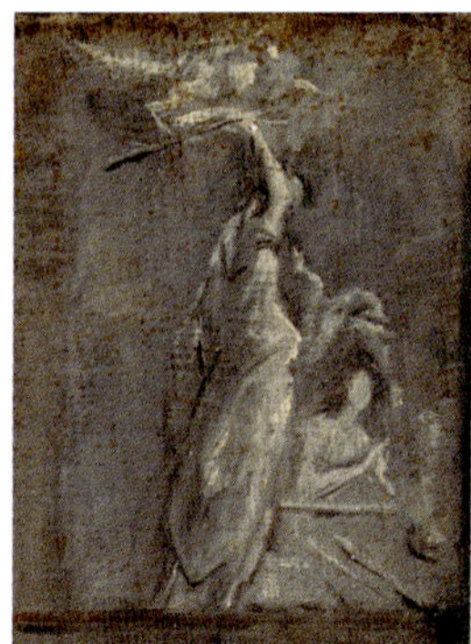

**50, 51** Details from *Christ driving the Traders from the Temple*

seven deadly sins), although his facial expression remains calm. It is his bodily action that gives away his anger. In his right hand he holds a whip made from rope, poised to strike at the half-clothed figure in yellow on the left, who is holding up his arm and backing away. This is not the peaceful Christ whom we have encountered thus far. El Greco depicted a moment from the Gospels where Christ drove out traders selling animals for sacrifice, furious that the temple was being used for commerce rather than worship. While he was working in Venice, El Greco started painting a number of versions of the scene in which traders and moneychangers are desecrating the Temple of Jerusalem, the heart of the Jewish faith.[86] Here, El Greco includes a sculptural relief of Adam and Eve's expulsion from the Garden of Eden to the left of the arch, emphasising the sinfulness of the traders [50]. Opposite the traders Christ's apostles stand beneath another relief that underscores their piety. It shows Abraham about to sacrifice Isaac following God's instructions, as an angel stops him mid-act [51]. We already encountered that exact scene in *The Presentation in the Temple* [40]. But what about the protagonist in *Christ driving the Traders from the Temple*? We have seen that wrath (*ira*) is a sin, but here Christ's anger seems righteous. The traders are committing a worse sin than he is, and Christ's wrath seems justified.

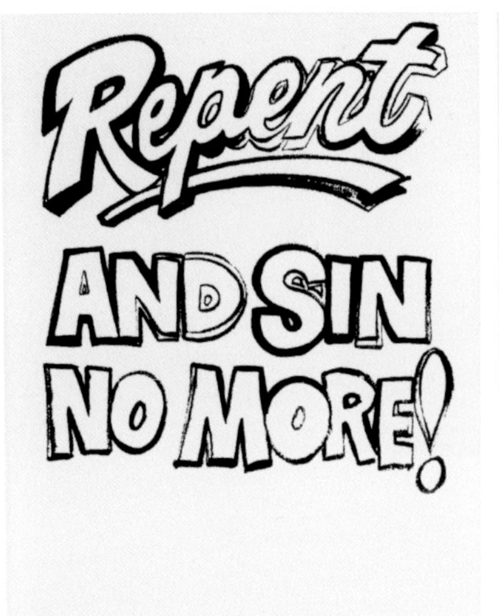


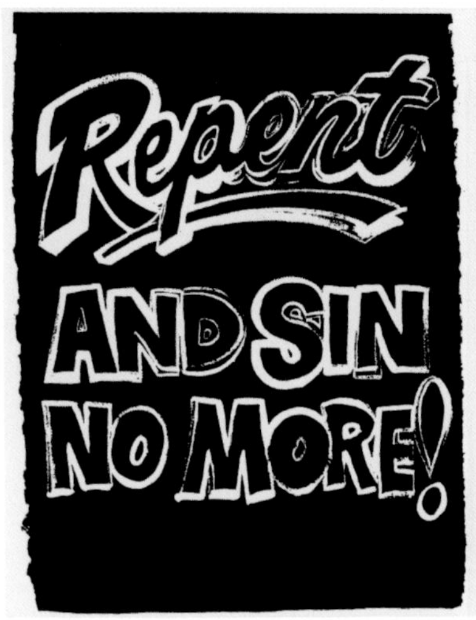


**52** Andy Warhol (1928–1987), *Repent, and Sin No More! (Positive and Negative)*, 1985–6. Acrylic paint and silkscreen on canvas, each 50.8 × 40.6 cm. Ed Freedman, Los Angeles, CA, USA.

## PAINTING AND REPENTING

As Saint Anthony was burdened in Annibale Carracci's picture [48], human beings have been burdened by sins in many guises. Be that as it may, there is a way that people can rid themselves of their burden. Repentance is the first step to salvation, and is part of many of the world's religions. Human beings do not have to wait until the afterlife to repent, like the souls in Dante's Purgatory carrying boulders on their backs. Repentance is possible in life too. To repent is to feel or express sincere regret or remorse about one's wrongdoing or sin. It is often a first stage that might bring about better things. Just as sinning is often a choice – a product of free will – so too is repenting. Repentance is part of everyday life as much as doing something bad is.

Few artists have addressed repentance as directly as Andy Warhol in some of his last paintings. Why paint a picture if you can paint the word? In some ways this is a rather Protestant thing to do. Followers of Luther, for instance, made 'word altarpieces' with the text of the Ten Commandments, Gospels, the Lord's Prayer and so on.[87] Warhol's worded works are not altarpieces; they are in fact based on pamphlets handed to the artist on the streets of New York. Their messages are

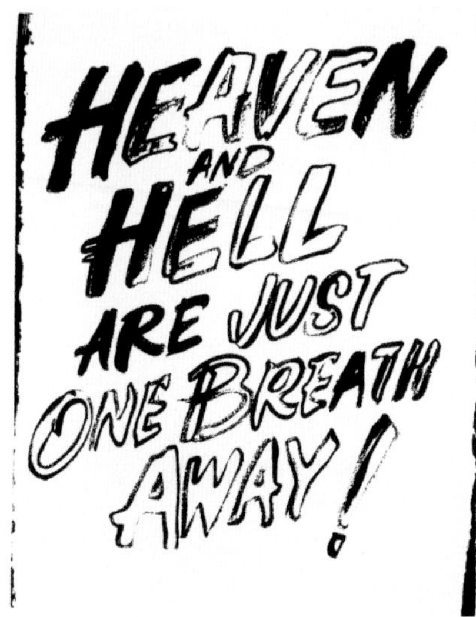


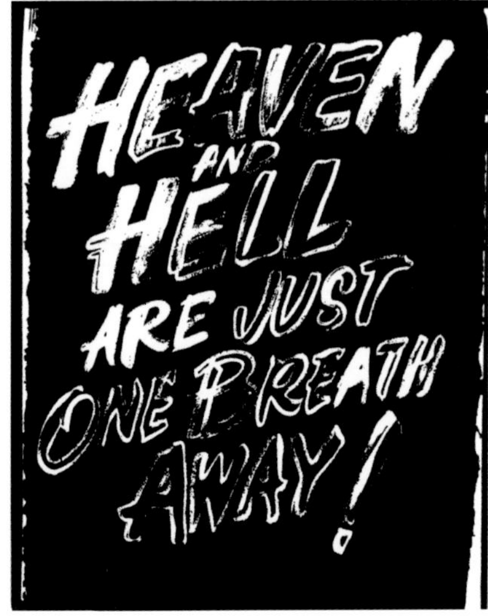


**53** Andy Warhol (1928–1987), *Heaven and Hell are Just One Breath Away! (Positive)*, 1985–6. Acrylic paint and silkscreen on canvas, 50.8 × 40.6 cm. Private collection.

**54** Andy Warhol (1928–1987), *Heaven and Hell are Just One Breath Away! (Negative)*, 1985–6. Acrylic paint and silkscreen on canvas, 50.8 × 40.6 cm. Private collection.

decidedly unambiguous: *Repent, and Sin No More!* [52] and *Heaven and Hell are Just One Breath Away!* [53, 54]. Furthermore, they exist in both 'positive' and 'negative' versions. The positive ones show black letters on a white background; the negatives white letters on a black background, inversing the extremes of the tonal range – everything is literally and metaphorically very black and white. Pamphlets such as these are still handed out every day across cities and towns around the world. One example that was recently handed to the author on Trafalgar Square right outside the National Gallery proclaims: *Jesus is for Real!*

Although painting words might traditionally be associated with Protestantism, Warhol was in fact a practising Catholic. This is perhaps a surprising fact about an artist who is associated with New York's more excessive side in the American avant-garde art scene of the 1960s to 1980s.[88] Warhol was never particularly open about his faith, and *Repent* and *Heaven and Hell* were not shown during his lifetime.[89] The art historian John Richardson addressed Warhol's Catholicism in his eulogy for his friend at St Patrick's Cathedral in New York in 1987, revealing 'a side of his character that he hid from all but his closest friends'.[90] *Repent, and Sin No More!* presents a clear message that we should all adhere to, and emphasises a choice. *Heaven and Hell are Just One Breath Away!* signals the possible ramifications of this choice.

Warhol's use of white and black in his 'pamphlet paintings' plays on the moral symbolism of light and darkness. For instance, consider Christ's words in this passage from the Gospel of John (3: 17–21):

> Indeed, God did not send the Son into the world to condemn the world, but in order that the world might be saved through him. Those who believe in him are not condemned; but those who do not believe are condemned already, because they have not believed in the name of the only Son of God. And this is the judgment, that the light has come into the world, and people loved darkness rather than light because their deeds were evil. For all who do evil hate the light and do not come to the light, so that their deeds may not be exposed. But those who do what is true come to the light, so that it may be clearly seen that their deeds have been done in God.

Artists depicting religious subject matter have also used such tonal symbolism over many centuries.[91] Warhol emphasises the choice between light and dark, virtue and sin, that underlies these textual works. The light is not the fiery furnace appearing at the left margin of Teniers's painting [see 38]. It is the promise of salvation through repentance.

Choice is fundamental to works that address repentance, and Paolo Veronese painted the exact moment of a choice being made in *The Conversion of Mary Magdalene* [55]. Saint Mary Magdalene is strongly associated with repentance, and the so-called 'Penitent Magdalene' has been a popular subject among painters. Unlike the rich man in Teniers's painting, Mary's penance arrived in time, although many accounts of her life describe her pursuing a life of riches. *The Golden Legend*, the popular thirteenth-century compendium of saints' lives, paints a crude picture of her early existence:

> Magdalene, then, was very rich, and sensuous pleasure keeps company with great wealth. Renowned as she was for her beauty and her riches, she was no less known for the way she

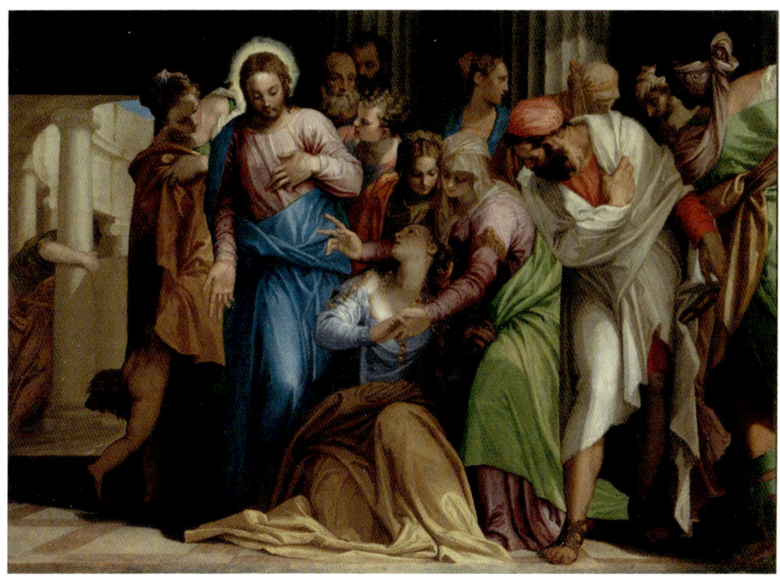

**55** Paolo Veronese (1528–1588), *The Conversion of Mary Magdalene*, about 1548. Oil on canvas, 117.5 × 163.5 cm. The National Gallery, London

> gave her body to pleasure – so much that her proper name was forgotten and she was commonly called 'the sinner'.[92]

Veronese's picture shows how Mary is converted by her encounter with Christ in the Jewish Temple and turns from a sinful life to a life of piety.[93] Veronese depicts the powerful moment when a sinner relinquishes the worldly for the spiritual with great attention to detail, to the extent of the fine linen gown trimmed with gold and studded with pearls.[94] Mary's rapture is palpable as she stares up at Christ. We are now looking at one of Christ's most devoted disciples, the 'sinner' moniker a thing of the past.

Mary Magdalene, and all human beings for that matter, are burdened by the debt of sin, with one exception. The doctrine of the Immaculate Conception states that God preserved the Virgin Mary from the taint of Original Sin from the moment that she was conceived, unlike the rest of us. The doctrine was controversial and much debated. For a long time, the Franciscans were staunch defenders and the Dominicans staunch opponents of the Virgin's sinlessness, and it was only officially proclaimed as dogma in 1854.[95] The constitution of Pope Pius IX, who was pope when the doctrine was finally accepted, states the following on the Immaculate Conception:

> … so the most holy Virgin, united with him by a most intimate and indissoluble bond, was, with him and through him, eternally at enmity with the evil serpent, and most completely triumphed over him, and thus crushed his head with her immaculate foot.[96]

It seems possible that the Pope had Caravaggio's picture where Mary and the infant Christ jointly trample the snake in mind [see 10]. Perhaps the most expressive depiction of the sinless Virgin Mary is Diego Velázquez's *Immaculate Conception* [56]. It might be surprising that a full-length depiction of a saint can carry with it the weight of an entire doctrine, and yet it does.[97] This type of picture of the Virgin Mary as 'Immaculate' became very popular in Spain, and Velázquez painted a striking example. She is standing on the moon with the sun behind her head, as is the custom, with a crown of 12 stars. The evocative accoutrements come from the Book of Revelation (12: 1), which describes such a vision at the time of the Apocalypse: 'A great portent appeared in heaven: a woman clothed with the sun, with the moon under her feet, and on her head a crown of twelve stars.' Below her, in the moonlit landscape, are more symbols traditionally associated with her purity: the garden, fountain, temple and the ship visible through a translucent moon.

Velázquez's model appears to have been a teenage girl with rosy cheeks and fair hair who looks like she just stepped off Seville's streets, contrasting with the complexities of the theology underlying this picture or at least making it very real and understandable. Velázquez painted it for the Shod Carmelite convent in Seville, together with a companion piece also housed in the National Gallery, *Saint John the Evangelist on the Island of Patmos* [57]. John the Evangelist was long believed to be the author of the Book of Revelation and therefore the one to describe the vision of the woman crowned with stars equated with the Immaculate Virgin, appearing in the top left corner. The inhabitants of the Carmelite house of Nuestra Señora del Carmen were active supporters of the doctrine of the Immaculate Conception

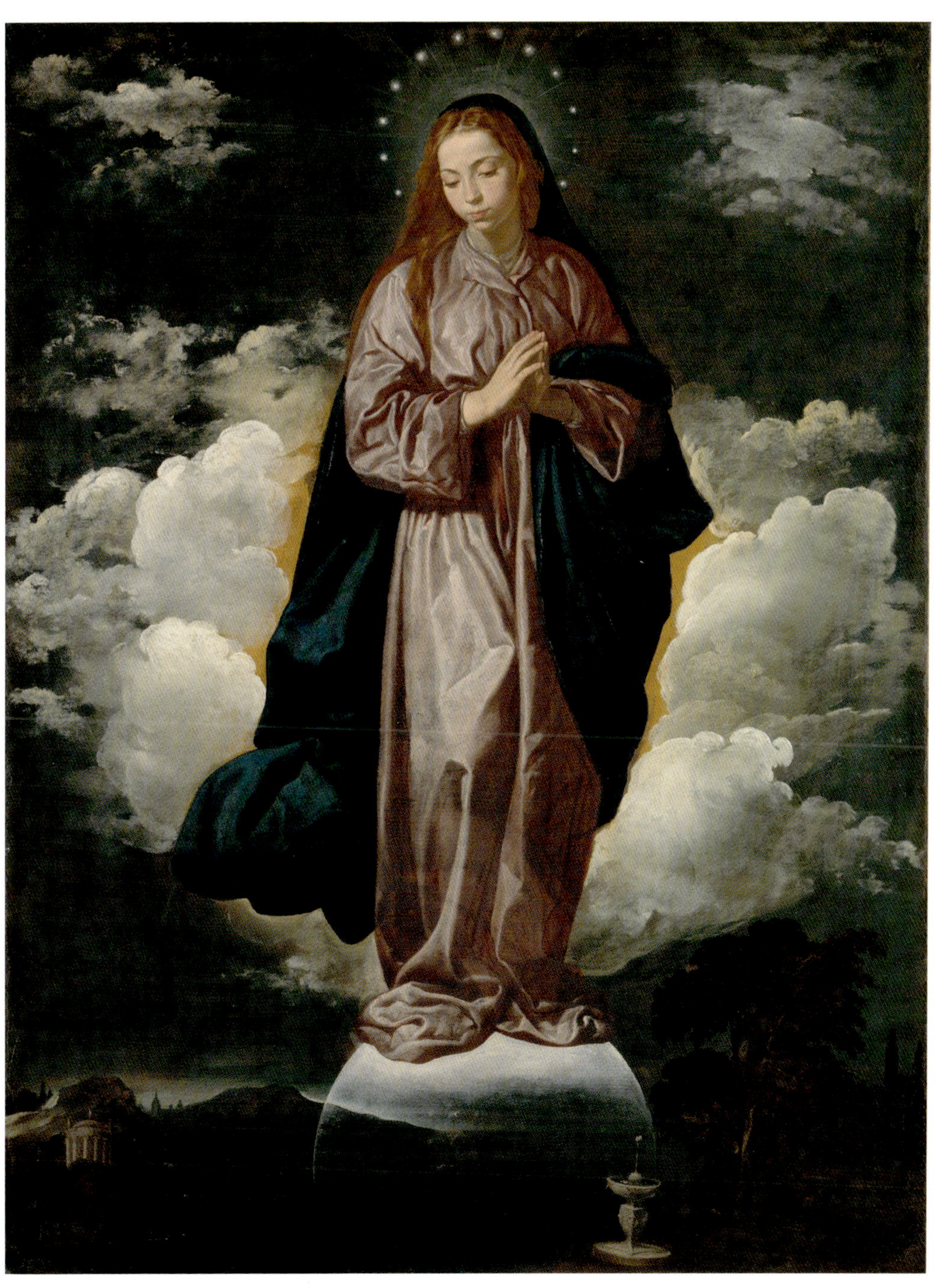

**56** Diego Velázquez (1599–1660), *The Immaculate Conception*, 1618–19. Oil on canvas, 135 × 101.6 cm. The National Gallery, London

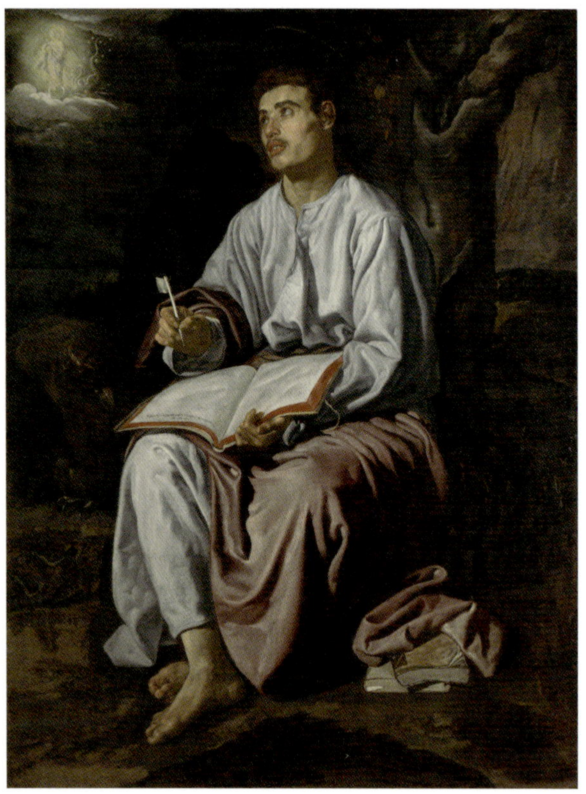

**57** Diego Velázquez (1599–1660), *Saint John the Evangelist on the Island of Patmos*, 1618–19. Oil on canvas, 135.5 × 102.2 cm. The National Gallery, London

in Seville, and the Carmelite Order had professed an ancient devotion to Mary's sinlessness.[98] It is tempting to think that the young Velázquez used a young model to underline his painting's message of the Immaculacy and purity of the Virgin Mary.

God did not bless all of us with the gift of Immaculacy. We have had to be creative in addressing our sinful existence. Perhaps humankind's most imaginative way to 'deal' with sin is the scapegoat. It is a term used in day-to-day conversation. A scapegoat is a person who is blamed for the wrongdoings, mistakes or faults of others, especially for reasons of expediency. A scapegoat is someone to blame. The origin of the term is found in the Old Testament Book of Leviticus, in a passage that describes an ancient Jewish ritual on the Day of Atonement (Yom

Kippur). First, the priest was to sacrifice one goat within the Holy of Holies whose blood was a sin offering to make atonement for the people of Israel. The second goat in this ritual is called the scapegoat, described in Leviticus 16: 20–2:

> When he has finished atoning for the holy place and the tent of meeting and the altar, he shall present the live goat. Then Aaron shall lay both his hands on the head of the live goat, and confess over it all the iniquities of the people of Israel, and all their transgressions, all their sins, putting them on the head of the goat, and sending it away into the wilderness by means of someone designated for the task. The goat shall bear on itself all their iniquities to a barren region; and the goat shall be set free in the wilderness.

The goat was a metaphorical 'beast of burden', in the way that sin was understood to be a burden or weight, rather like Botticelli's boulder-carriers. It carried the sins of the people away into the wilderness. A painterly depiction of the scapegoat is rare, but the British Pre-Raphaelite painter William Holman Hunt was fascinated by the story and painted the subject twice. In a letter from 1854 he remarked: '... it has never before been done. It is so full of meaning ... and it is so simple ...'[99] The smaller first version of *The Scapegoat*, now in Manchester Art Gallery, is a riotous display of colour and dramatic light effects [58].[100] There is little else like it. Holman Hunt – a devout Christian – executed the picture on the shores of the Dead Sea in the middle of the nineteenth century.[101] The painter had gone on an intellectual quest to experience the origins of Christianity first-hand. The dark goat staring out at us looks exhausted, as if it cannot take our sins away any further. The skull of what appears to be an ibex sticks out of the marshes on the left, echoing the goat's inevitable fate. The red wool around the goat's horns has special significance [59]. Isaiah 1: 18 reads: 'Come now, let us argue it out, says the Lord: though your sins are like scarlet, they shall be like snow; though they are red like crimson, they shall become like wool.' The Manchester version of *The Scapegoat* includes the olive branch in the left foreground and the rainbow. The olive branch is the sign brought by the dove to Noah in Genesis 8 to show that the flood had begun to subside. The rainbow is a symbol from Genesis 9, where God's covenant

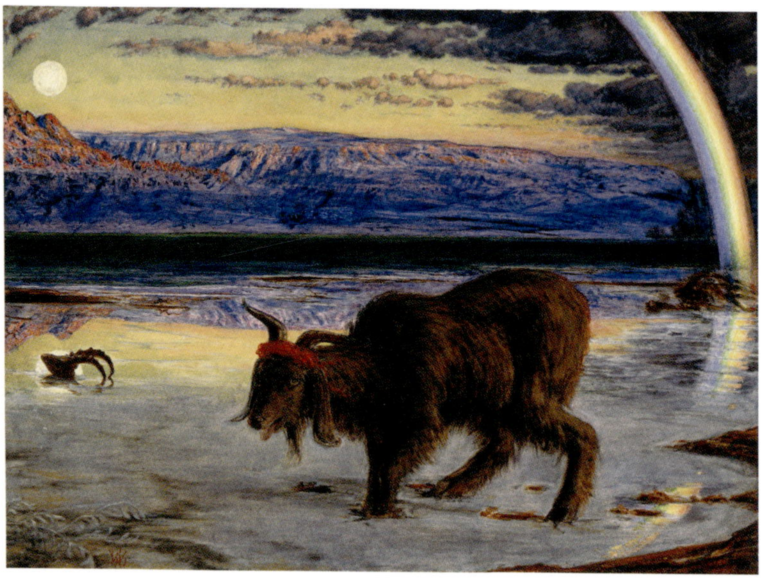

**58, 59** (opposite) William Holman Hunt (1827–1910), *The Scapegoat*, 1854–5. Oil on canvas, 33.7 × 45.9 cm. Manchester Art Gallery

with the people meant that there would never be another flood; that he would never destroy his creation again. Both the scapegoat and the goat that was sacrificed in the temple are sometimes considered precursors to Christ, 'sin offerings' of flesh and blood. For Christians, Christ's sacrifice was sufficient to restore God's relationship with humanity once and for all.

Most of us do not have a scapegoat to send into the wilderness. In that case the first step of penance is often confession. Confession is a formal way of saying sorry for one's sins in the hope of being forgiven for them. It usually involves being humbled in front of the witness of the confession, and is therefore the antidote to pride, *superbia*.[102] One picture in the National Gallery's collection depicts a miraculous case of such a confession to a priest, *The Mass of Saint Giles* [62]. It is an engrossing story. The panel is one of four surviving fragments of an altarpiece that showed the lives of various French saints, painted in or near Paris around the year 1500. The saint depicted here is Giles (or Aegidius), the priest performing Mass. More interesting, however, is the sinner kneeling in prayer at the altar, the Holy Roman Emperor Charlemagne. *The Golden Legend* summarises the event:

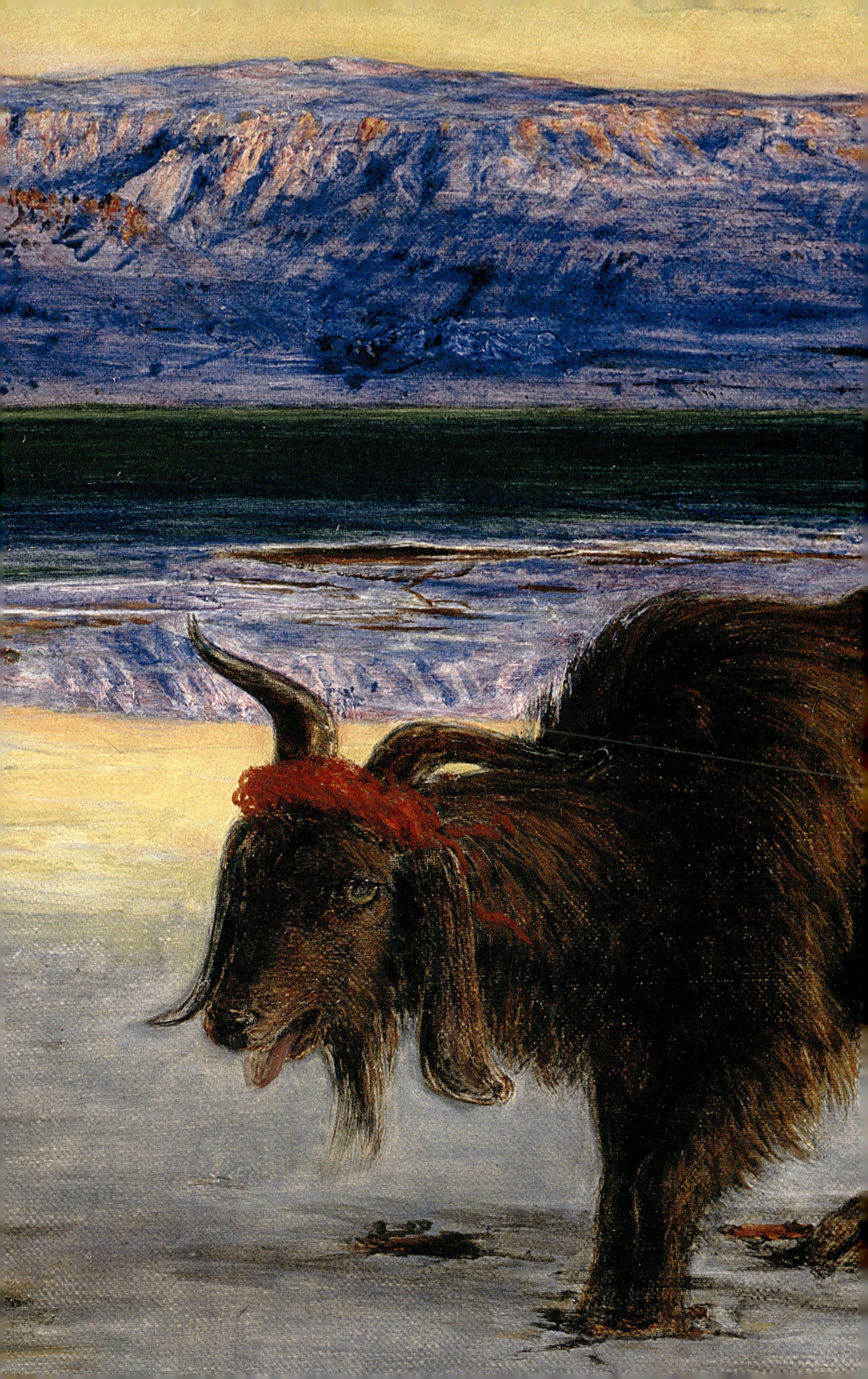

> … he [Charlemagne] had committed an enormous crime, which he dared not confess even to the saint himself. The following Sunday, while Giles was celebrating mass and praying for the king, an angel of the Lord appeared to him and deposited on the altar a scroll on which it was written that the king's sin was forgiven due to Giles's prayer, provided that the king was truly repentant, confessed his sin, and abstained from committing it thereafter.[103]

It seems that Giles's intercession spared Charlemagne the humbling often associated with confession. The amount of detail in *The Mass of Saint Giles* is extraordinary. Even the Latin text on the angel's note is legible [60]. It reads (in translation): 'By the merit of Giles, remission of sins is granted to Charles.'[104] The detail extends to the painting's setting, the Basilica of St-Denis. The magnificent altarpiece – originally an altar frontal – was given to the church by Charles the Bald and destroyed during the French Revolution.[105] The gold and gemstone object shows Christ enthroned holding a cross and a book below another cross, with smaller flanking saints holding books as they are crowned by angels. The surmounted cross, which is of an even earlier date, was believed to have been made by Saint Eligius and contained a relic of the True Cross. As Saint Giles holds up the consecrated bread

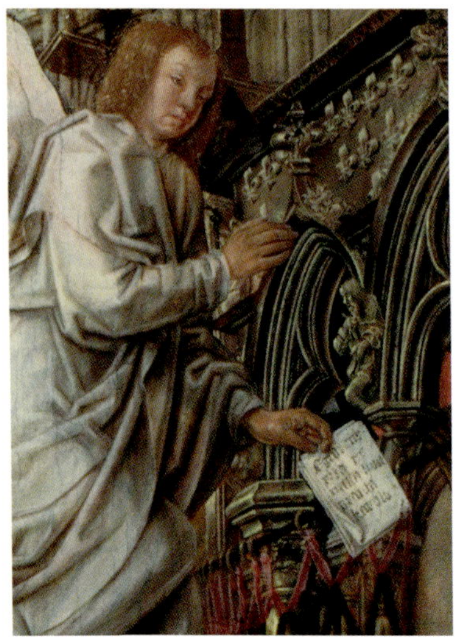

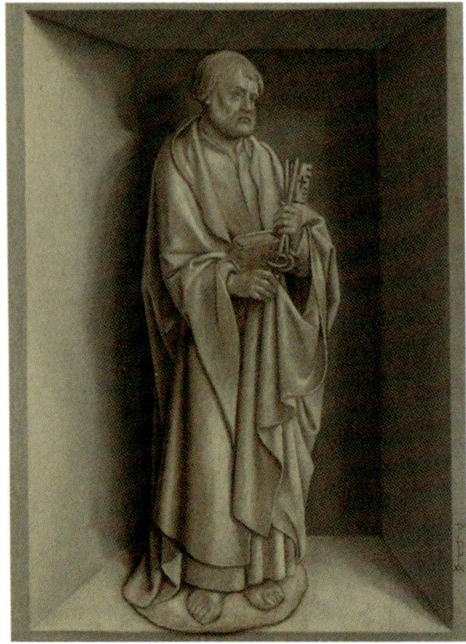

**60** Detail from *The Mass of Saint Giles*

**61** The reverse of *The Mass of Saint Giles*

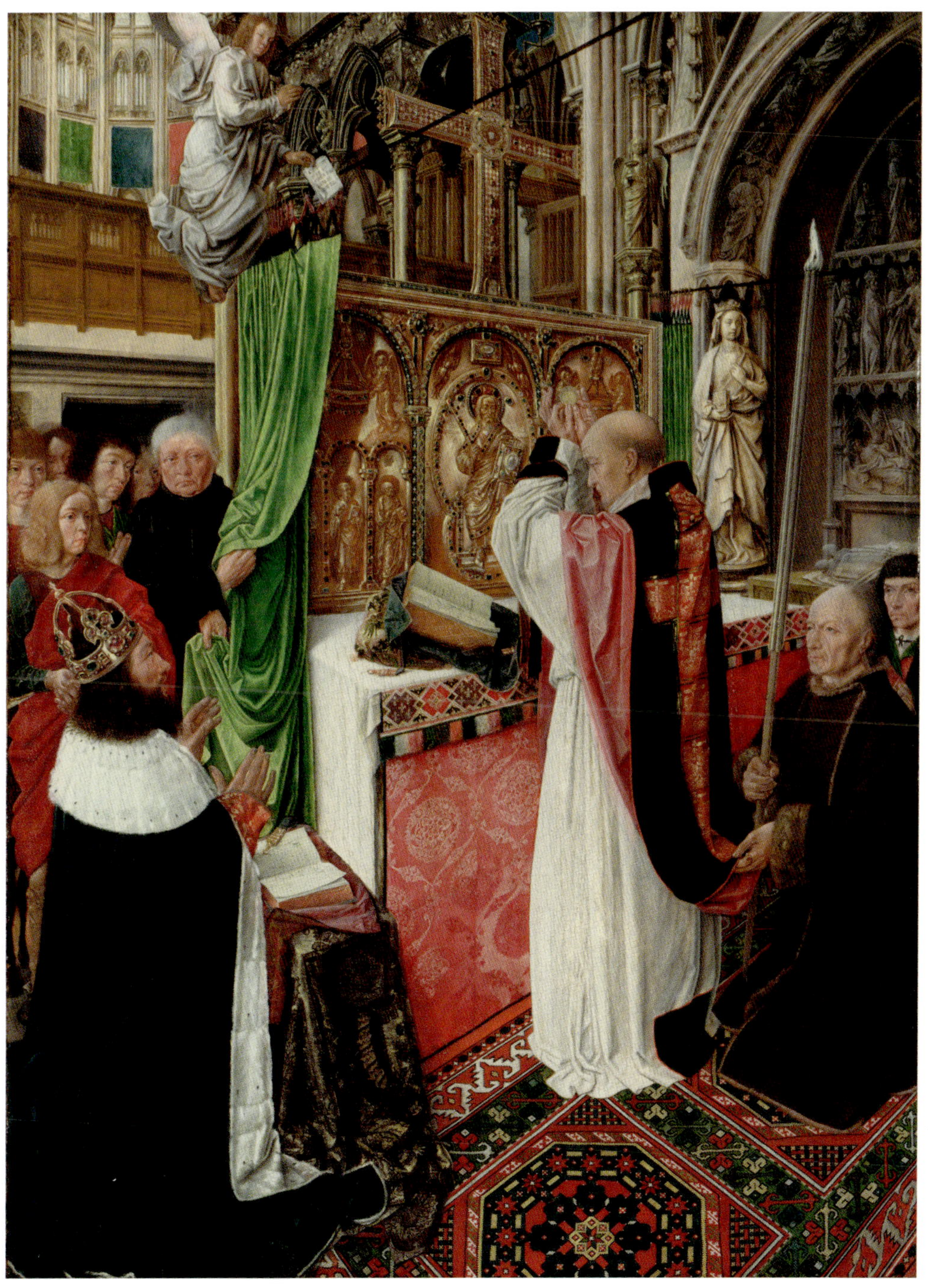

**62** Master of Saint Giles (active about 1500), *The Mass of Saint Giles*, about 1500. Oil on oak, 62.3 × 46 cm. The National Gallery, London

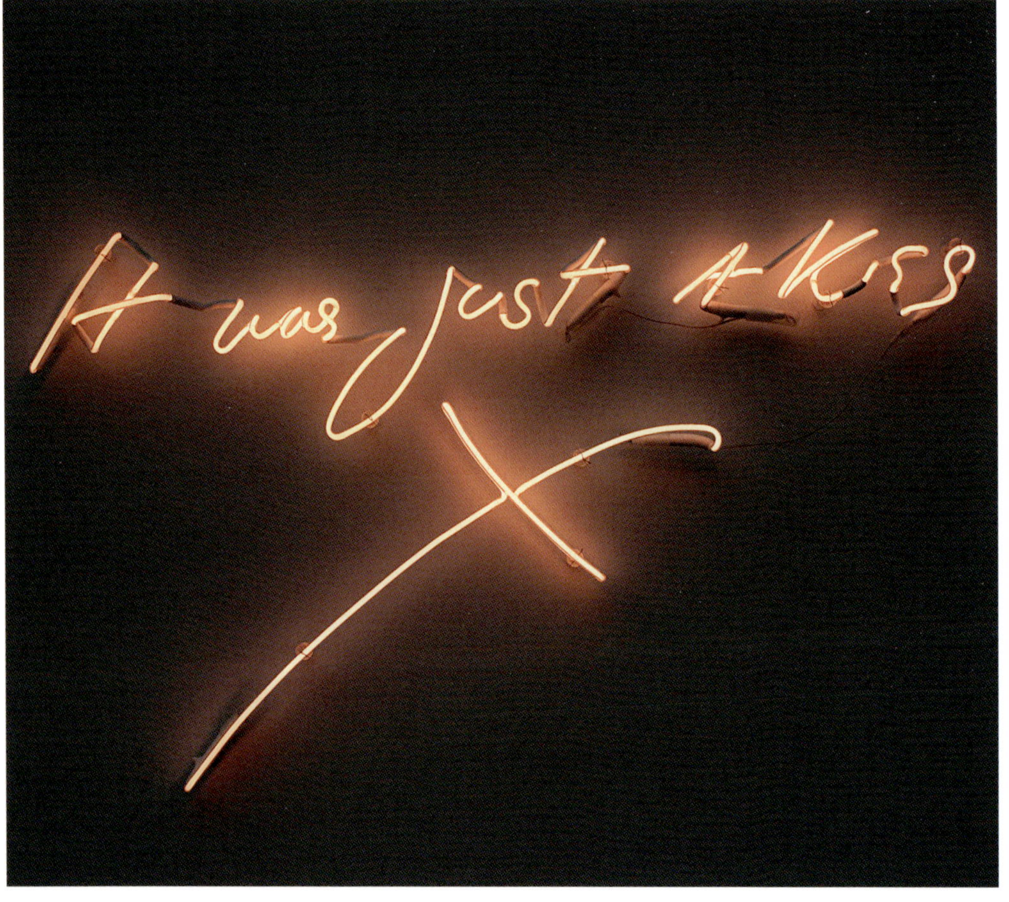


**63** Tracey Emin (born 1963), *It was just a kiss*, 2010.
Neon lights, 57.7 × 97.3 cm. Private collection.

of the Host – Christ's body – the Eucharistic ensemble is a reminder of who made it possible that Charlemagne's unspeakable sin was forgiven. Christ's physical presence in front of an altarpiece in *The Presentation in the Temple* [see 39] is in *The Mass of Saint Giles* replaced by his presence in the Host. Furthermore, *The Mass of Saint Giles* is a double-sided panel. On the reverse it shows Saint Peter holding the keys to heaven [61], a place to which Charlemagne doubtless hoped his confession would lead him without considerable detour. The fact that his sins were forgiven even before confessing them to Saint Giles surely speaks to confession's power. Later commentators claimed that Charlemagne's unspeakable sin had been necrophilia or incest.[106]

Everyone has confessed in their life, probably more often to a friend or family member than to a priest, although few will have experienced Charlemagne's preferential treatment. Artists too have been prone to confessing, even in their work. Tracey Emin's *It was just a kiss* could indeed be considered a confession [63], as could a large part of her oeuvre.[107] *It was just a kiss* – like Warhol's *Repent, and Sin No More!* and *Heaven and Hell are Just One Breath Away!* – is just that. It spells its title in bright neon letters, above a big 'X' in the same medium. The 'X' is another kiss, or a simplified signature. The whole ensemble appears to be 'written' in a rushed handwriting, enforcing the association with the personal, something scribbled on a piece of paper. Could one imagine such a piece of paper replacing the one delivered by the angel in *The Mass of Saint Giles* [60]? *It was just a kiss* could be words spoken to a lover, a friend, or even to a priest in a confessional. If that last part seems far-fetched, Emin's *For You* was installed in Liverpool Cathedral in 2008 [64].[108] It reads 'I Felt You And I Knew You Loved me'. The lower-

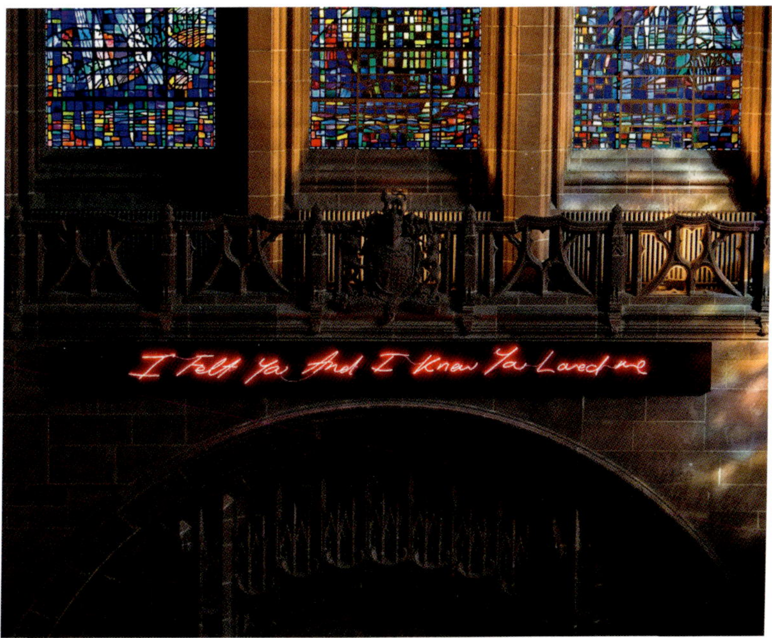


**64** Tracey Emin, *For You*, 2008.
Neon lights. Liverpool Cathedral

case 'm' in 'me' could be interpreted as Emin's expression of humility. The possibilities of that text gain new currency situated above the west door of a cathedral, below towering stained-glass windows. And maybe *It was just a kiss* does too, in the context of confession, and within the story of sin's art history.

Emin has never shied away from the personal and problematic in her work, which addresses sex, sexual abuse, pregnancies and abortions. Her neon messages range from the romantic (*I Never Stopped Loving You*) to the explicitly sexual.[109] *It was just a kiss* might be among her most ambiguous confessions. The phrase means something different to a long-term partner than it does to a hopeful suitor. It has connotations of both betrayal and dismissal, but it can be teasing too. Thinking back to two other pictures in this story, *It was just a kiss* becomes even more ambiguous. Ugolino di Nerio's painting of *The Betrayal of Christ* definitely does not show 'just' a kiss [see 43]. Judas' betrayal set events in motion on a par with Adam and Eve's first sin (Matthew 26: 48–9): 'Now the betrayer had given them a sign, saying, "The one I will kiss is the man; arrest him." At once he came up to Jesus and said, "Greetings, Rabbi!" and kissed him.'

Bronzino's *Allegory* was not 'just' a kiss to the painter and his circle of artists and humanists, or for Francis I of France [65]. It was a kiss with many intellectual and sexual connotations, something to be enjoyed and to be talked about. For the Victorian public who found the painting 'improper', they definitely did not consider the kiss between Venus and Cupid 'just' a kiss. And yet maybe, for many of those who look at it today, Bronzino's picture is 'just' a kiss.

**65** Detail from *An Allegory with Venus and Cupid*, p. 33

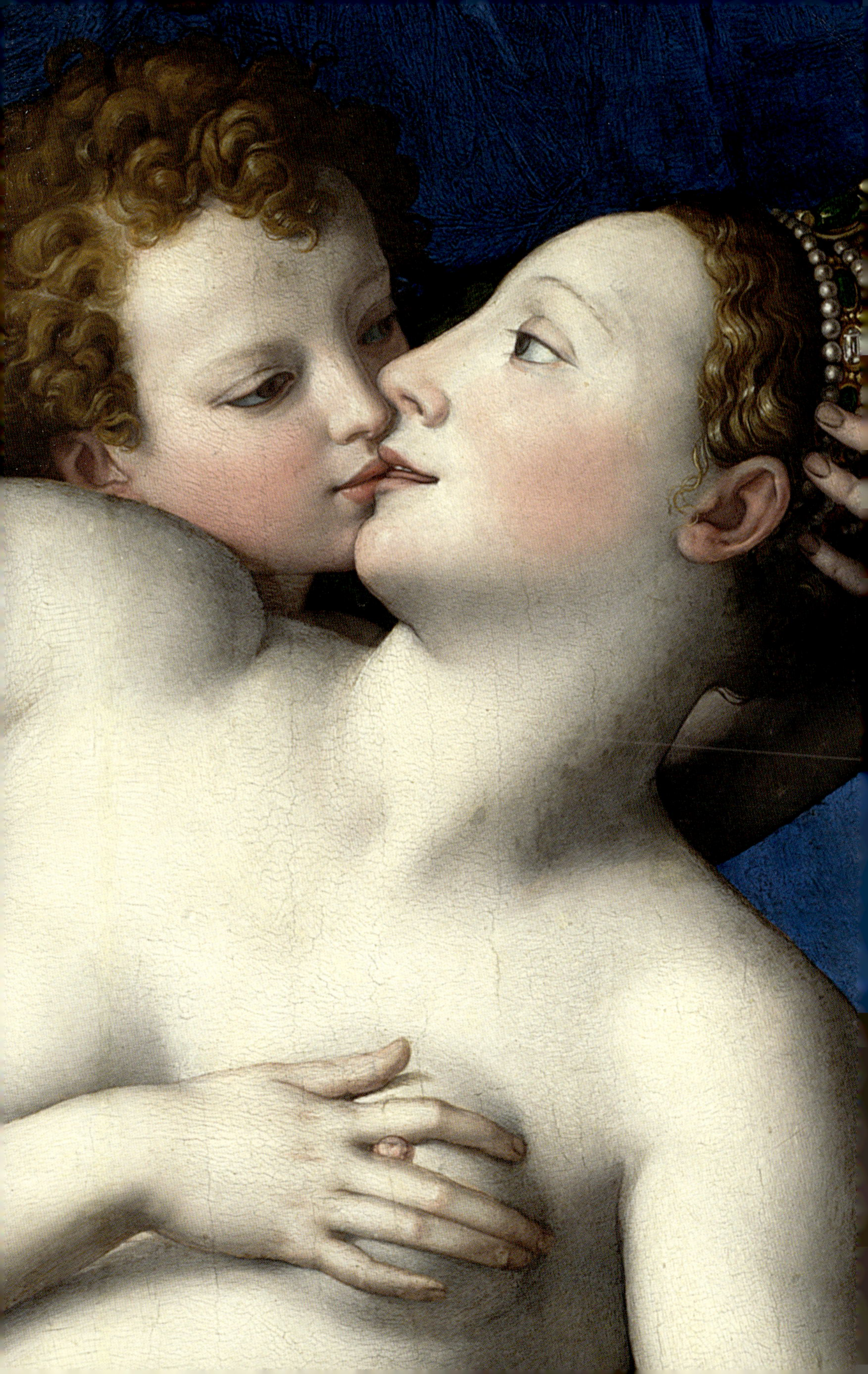

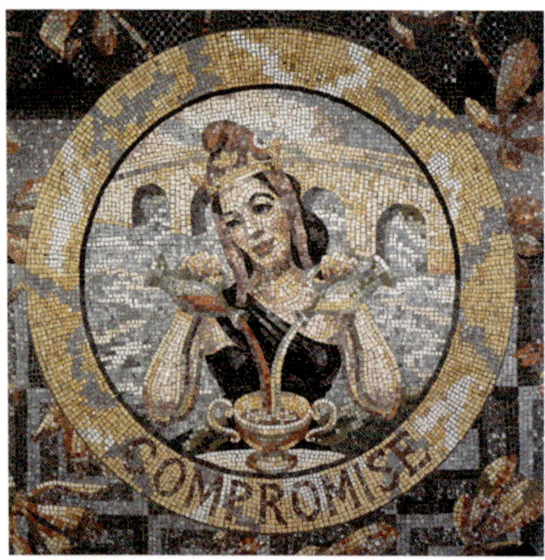


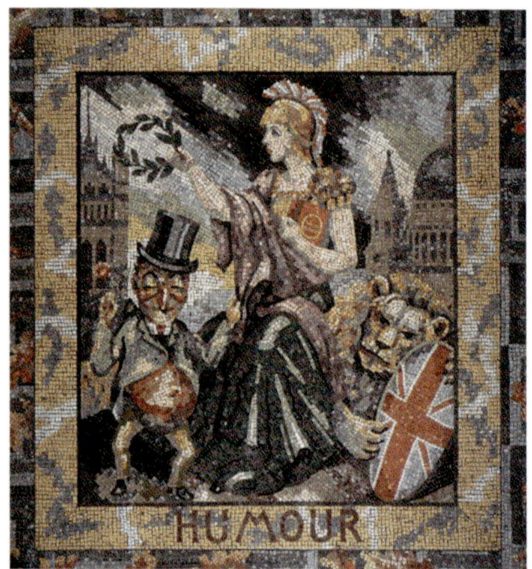


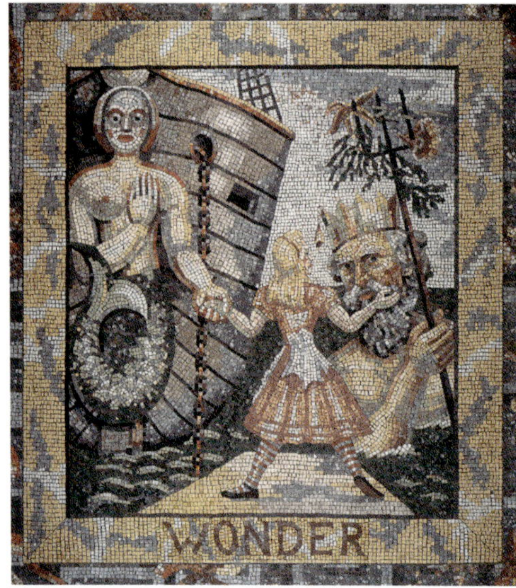


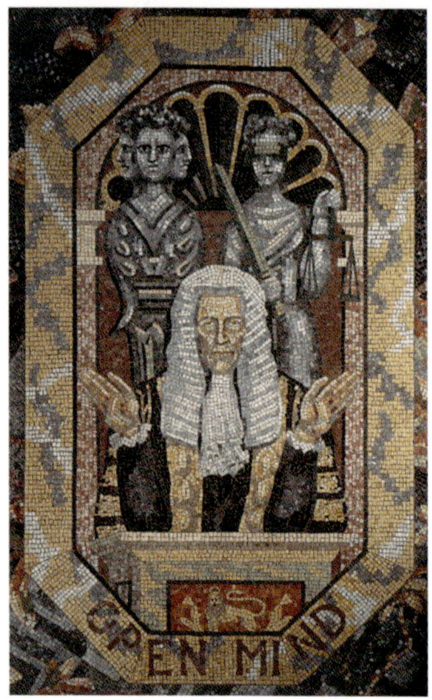


**66–9** Boris Anrep (1885–1969), *The Modern Virtues: Compromise, Humour, Wonder* and *Open Mind,* 1952. Mosaic. The National Gallery, London

## THE FIRST TO THROW A STONE

Visitors to the National Gallery often walk over Boris Anrep's mosaics on the steps and landings inside the Portico Entrance vestibule, leading to the Central Hall and Room 1. On the whole, they do not pay much attention to what is underneath their feet. The mosaics in the west vestibule were completed on 31 May 1928 and show *The Labours of Life*; *The Pleasures of Life* in the east vestibule were finished on 13 November 1929, followed by *The Awakening of the Muses* in 1933.[110] Anrep's mosaics are highly idiosyncratic interpretations of traditional subjects. Among the *Pleasures*, for instance, one finds a Christmas pudding and cricket. Among the *Muses* there is the traditional pairing of Bacchus, associated with 'sinful' things such as wine and loose inhibitions, with Apollo to his right, representing a more virtuous side. Most figures are personifications of specific attributes, using portraits of people from Anrep's circle of acquaintances or well known from public life: the art critic Clive Bell is Bacchus, while the writer Sir Osbert Sitwell appears as Apollo.[111] After the Second World War, under director Sir Kenneth Clark, a final set of mosaics was unveiled: *The Modern Virtues*.[112] It seems another highly personal list, which Anrep based on what he considered good qualities among the British population, including *Compromise*, *Humour*, *Wonder* and (an) *Open Mind* [66–9]. By extension, looking down at the mosaics, each one of us might ask ourselves: 'what are *my* virtues?'

Introspection is key to virtue *and* sin, and it is key to art. Rarely have introspection and self-reflection been painted more powerfully than in Pieter Bruegel the Elder's *Christ and the Woman taken in Adultery* [70]. Its compact size and monochromatic palette demand close examination.[113] The picture might be small, but Bruegel painted one of the most profound calls for introspection in human history. The group of onlookers on the picture's left-hand side are curious to see what Christ is writing on the ground with his finger: '*DIE SONDER SONDE IS / DIE*'. In Dutch, Bruegel's Christ writes the first words of the second half of John 8: 7. The completed statement resonates like few other pieces of scripture: 'Let anyone among you who is without sin be the first to throw a stone at her.'

The sentence forms the climax of an episode from the Gospels in which members of some Jewish sects had brought a woman accused of a sinful act to Christ, both to punish the woman and to test (and maybe trick) Christ, whom the members of the Jewish ruling council

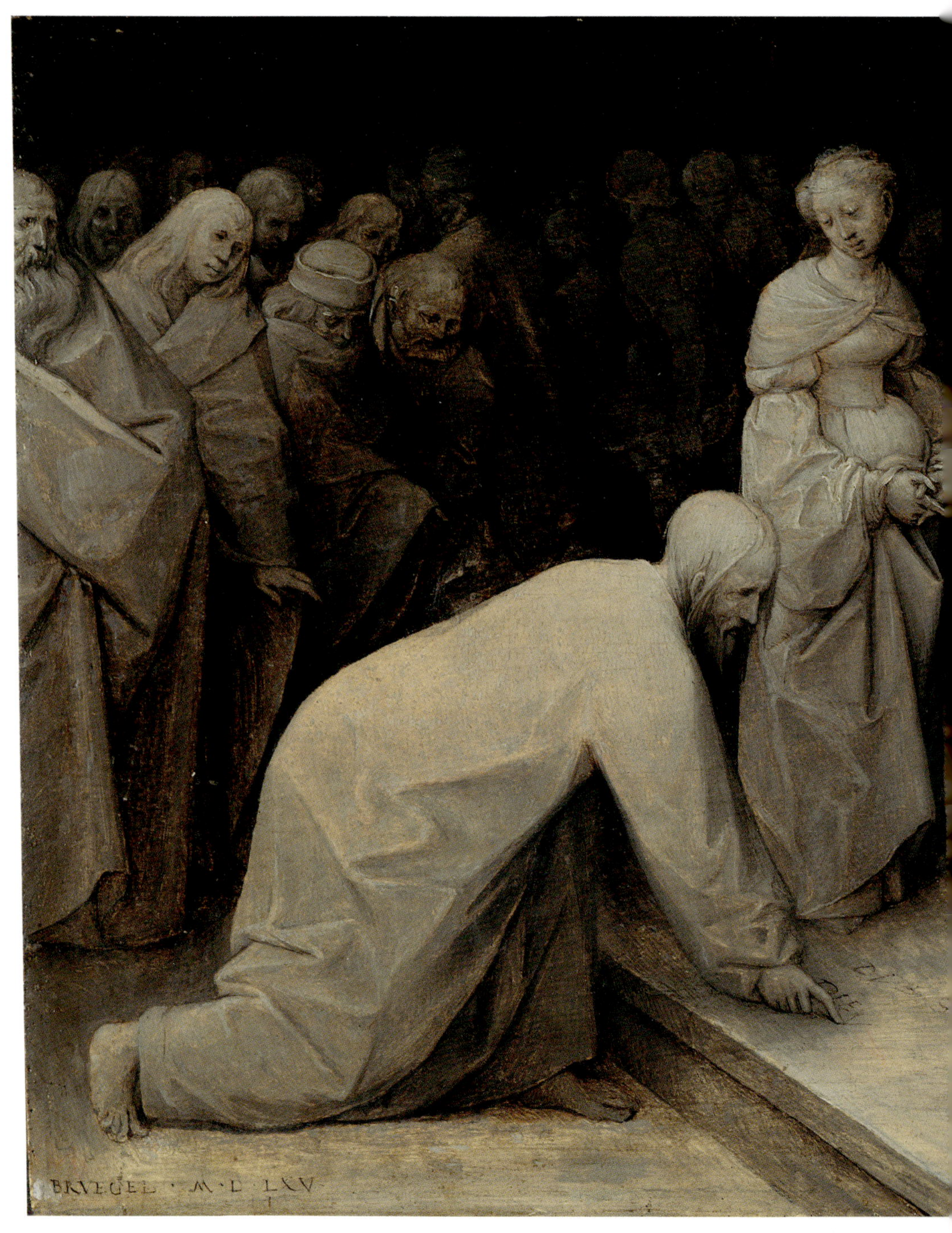

**70** Pieter Bruegel the Elder (active from 1550/1; died 1569), *Christ and the Woman taken in Adultery*, 1565. Oil on wood, 24.1 × 34.4 cm. The Samuel Courtauld Trust, The Courtauld Gallery, London on long term loan to the National Gallery

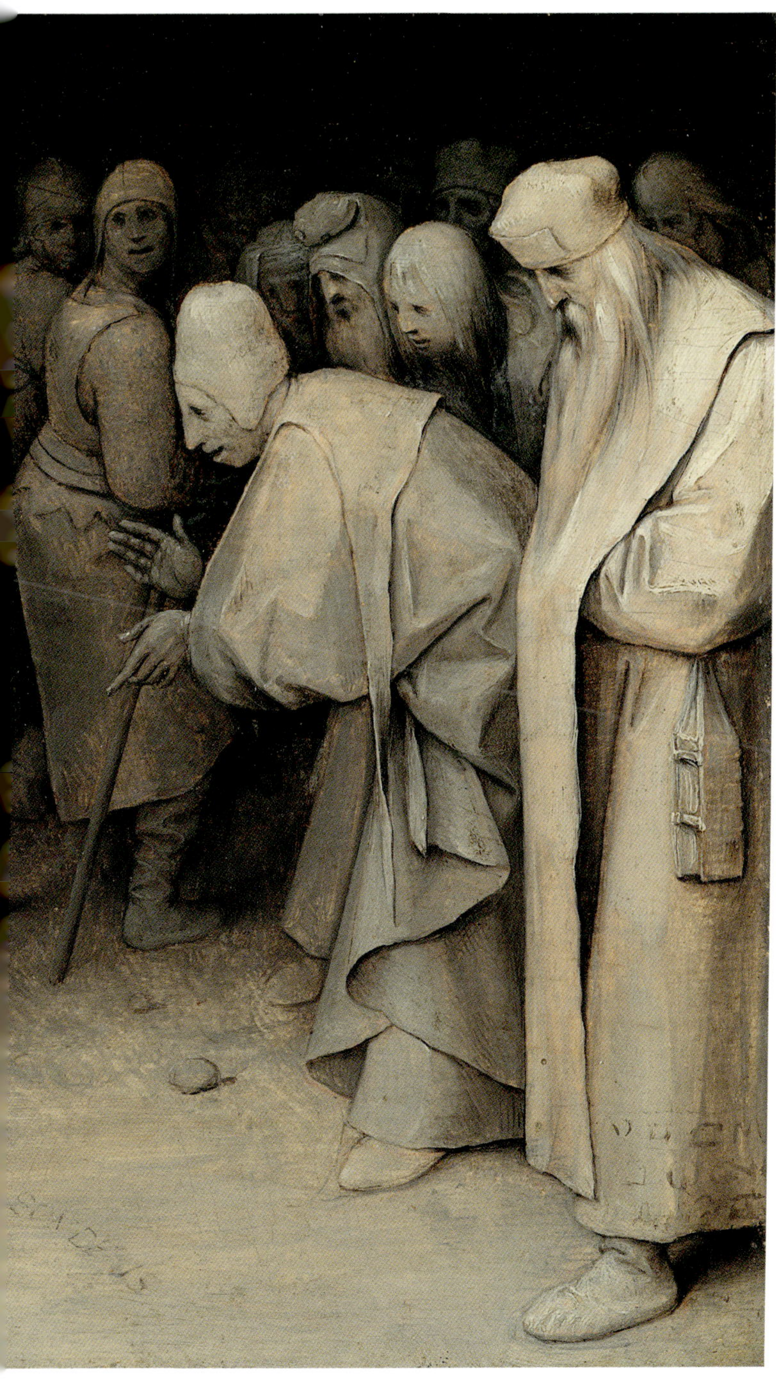

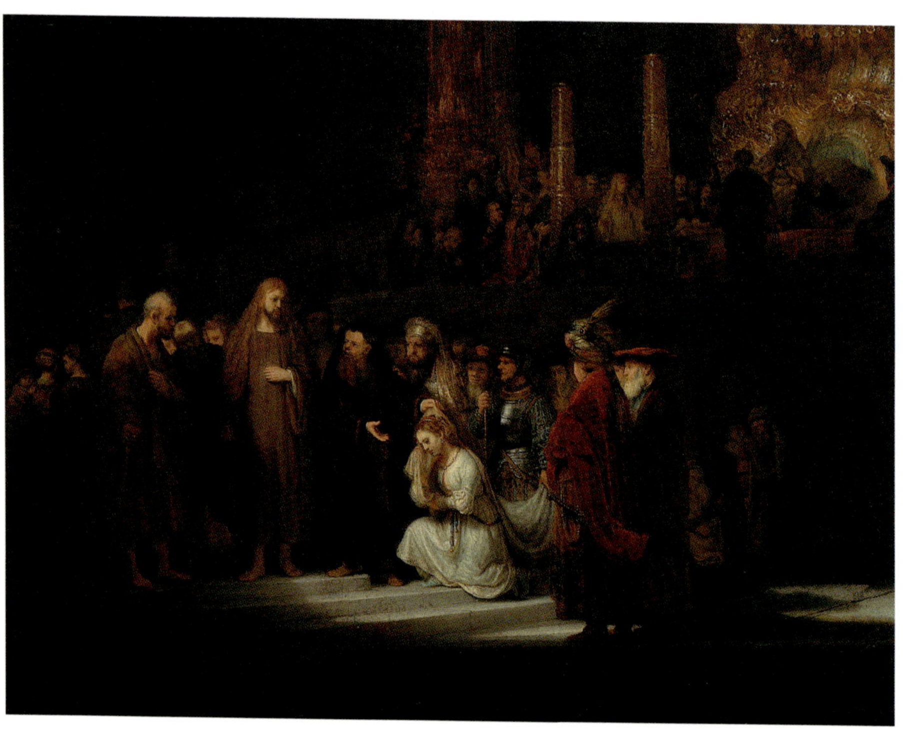

**71** Detail from Rembrandt (1606–1669), *The Woman taken in Adultery*, 1644. Oil on oak, 83.8 × 65.4 cm. The National Gallery, London

saw as a competitor: 'Teacher, this woman was caught in the very act of committing adultery. Now in the law Moses commanded us to stone such women. Now what do you say?' (4–5). Moses' laws were literally set in stone, and in Saint John's Gospel, Christ writes his reply humbly in the ground, beautifully depicted in Bruegel's stone-like picture.[114] It is difficult to underestimate the profundity of Christ's retort, and few statements about sin get to the heart of the matter quite so effectively.[115] It is perhaps no surprise that earlier in his career, Bruegel had designed a series of highly detailed allegorical engravings of *The Seven Deadly Sins*.[116] He also painted not one, but three versions of the *Tower of Babel*.[117] Sin seems to have mattered to Bruegel and his audience, and *Christ and the Woman taken in Adultery* is a deceptively simple picture that asks one of sin's most profound questions. Rembrandt's treatment of the same subject in the National Gallery's collection seems to leave us as viewers in suspense [71]. One of the male onlookers puts his finger to his lips as if hushing the crowd. Where Bruegel presents us with Christ's answer, Rembrandt leaves us waiting for Christ's mercy, as if he is interrogating the viewer. It makes us think about how we would answer such an accusation.

Maybe Ron Mueck's *Youth* asks a similar question [73]. In 2000 Mueck became the National Gallery's fifth Associate Artist, which involved a two-year residency in the Gallery, allowing the artist to respond to the collection.[118] This later sculpture particularly echoes some of the minute details found in the Gallery's Netherlandish collections. *Youth* has an obvious kinship to depictions of Christ, most notably through the boy's wound on his torso, which parallels one of the five 'Holy Wounds' that Christ suffered during his crucifixion.[119] Besides the four nail wounds on his hands and feet, Christ received a fifth wound on the right-hand side of his torso when he was pierced by the lance of a Roman soldier. *Youth* makes us think back to the Christ in the centre of Bosch's idiosyncratic tabletop [72], but also the dead Christ suspended on the Cross in Raphael's altarpiece [see 44].

Why is the young man bleeding, as he stands barefoot on his pedestal in his simple white T-shirt and jeans? The sculpture is thoroughly suggestive, and asks more questions than it answers. Many of these questions relate to sin. Ostensibly *Youth* is the victim of a stabbing, or is he in fact another Christ? The puzzled expression on his face does not necessarily provide an answer: victims of stabbings often only realise that they have been stabbed after the wound has been inflicted. Simultaneously *Youth*'s expression reminds us of saints: Saint Thomas the Apostle ('Doubting Thomas') famously only believed that Christ had risen from the dead and appeared in front of him after he could see and feel Christ's sacrificial wounds. And in the thirteenth century Saint Francis of Assisi received the stigmata – 'copies' of Christ's wounds – after having experienced a divine vision of the crucified Christ. Both Thomas and Francis must have experienced bafflement, just as *Youth*'s expression suggests. Maybe this expression reminds us of Adam in Cranach's painting too [see 5]. *Youth* asks questions about the sins of today's society. London's gang violence has led to a surge in knife crime, and many of its victims are young men. *Youth*'s ambiguity is meaningful and holds many possible answers. Is he another Christ or perhaps another scapegoat, burdened with the sins of others and left

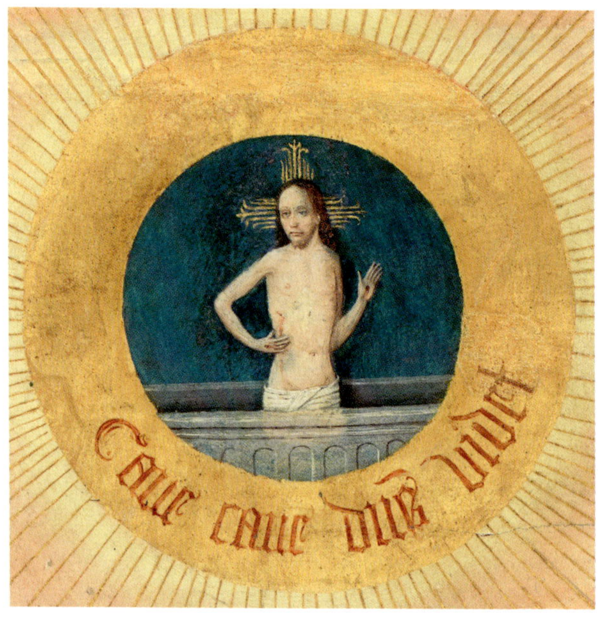

**72** Detail of Christ from *Table of the Seven Deadly Sins*, p. 41.
The inscription states: 'Beware, beware, the Lord sees.'

to die far away in a metaphorical 'wilderness'? Like Bruegel's Christ, *Youth* first and foremost demands an interrogation of our own sins and their consequences. Self-reflection in this sense not only encourages us to ask difficult questions, but can also lead to illuminating insights. Maybe Dante said it best:

> My lowered eyes caught sight of the clear stream,
> but when I saw myself reflected there,
> such shame weighed on my brow, my eyes drew back ...[120]

**73** Ron Mueck (born 1958), *Youth*, 2009.
Mixed media, 65 × 28 × 16 cm. Courtesy the artist

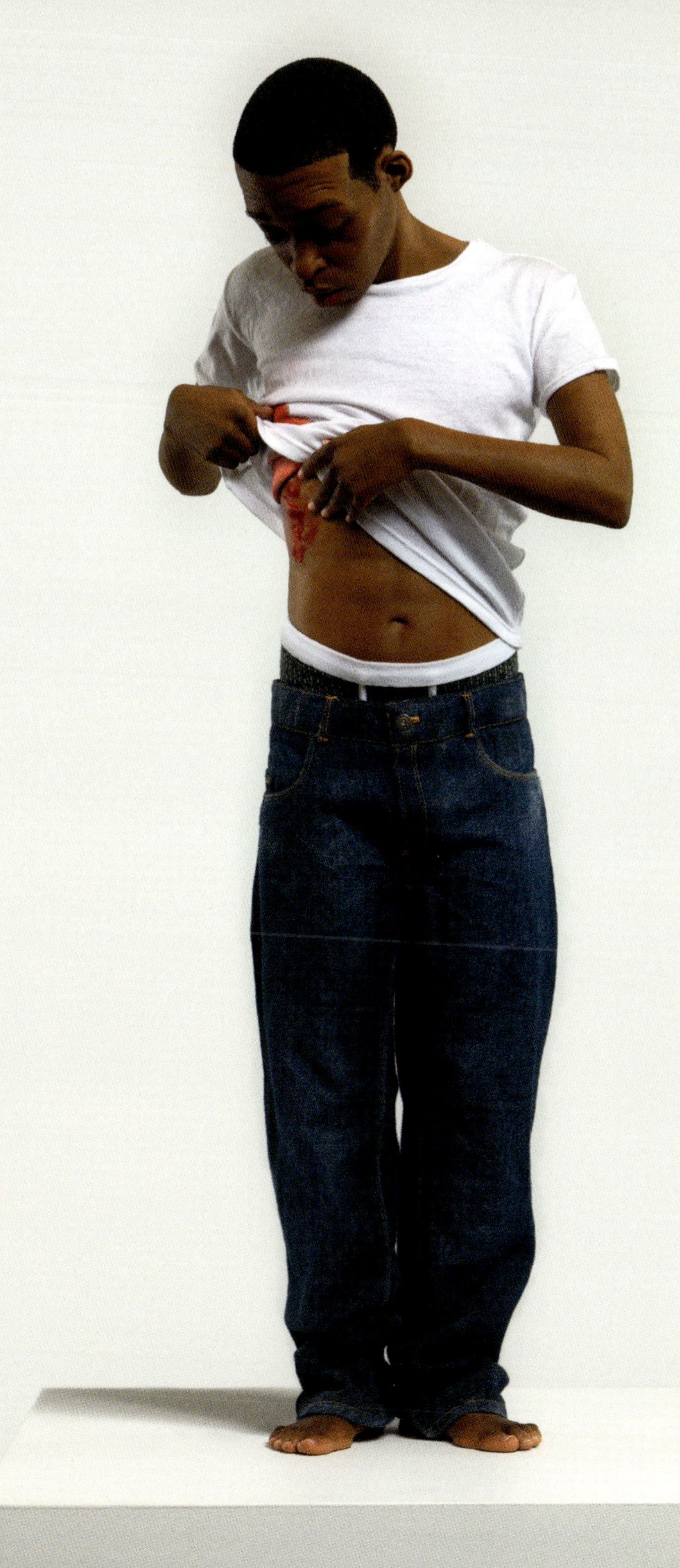

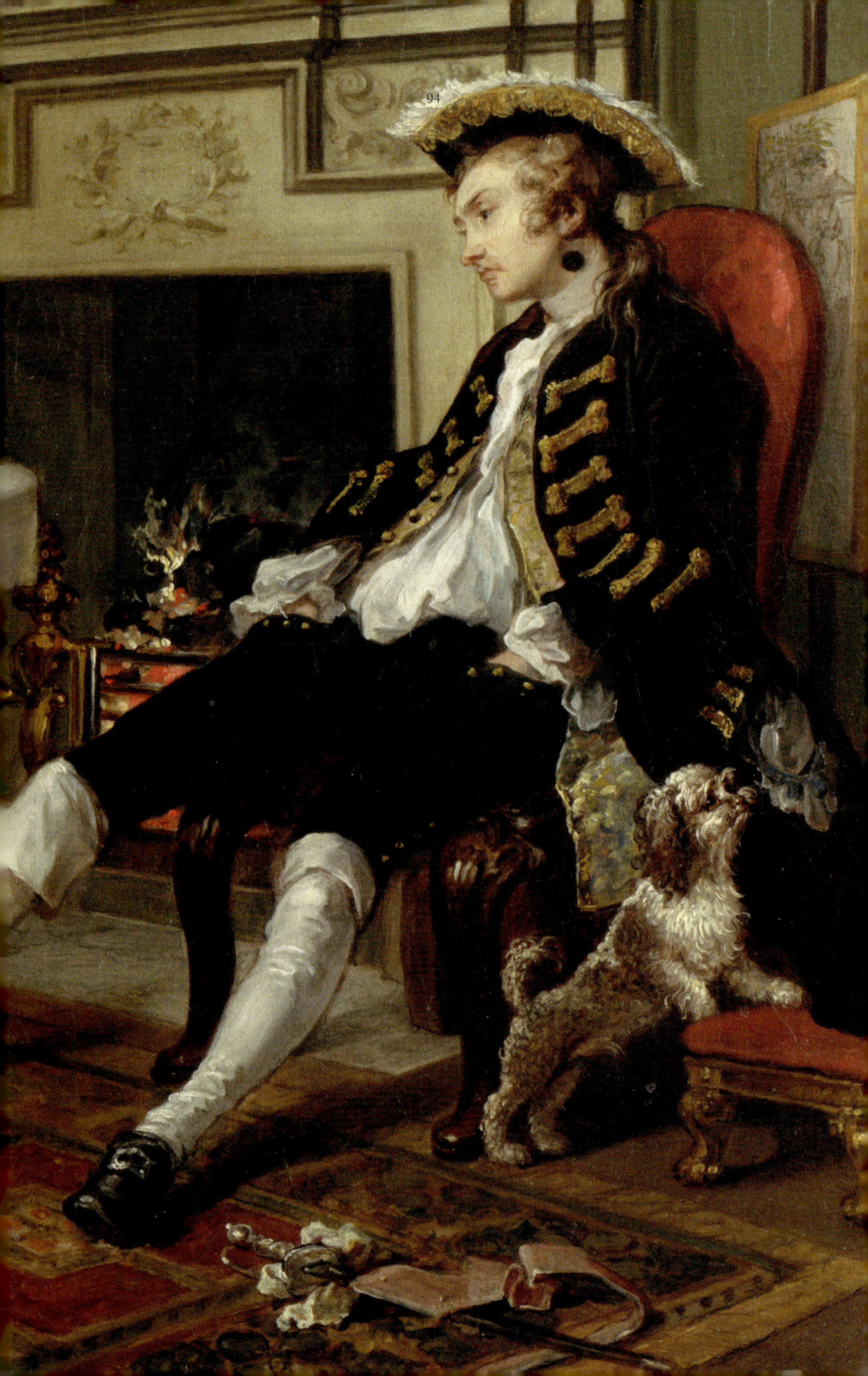

# NOTES

1 Twain 1894, p. 27.
2 The theologian Karl Barth gave a good example: 'Sin is that by which man as we know him is defined, for we know nothing of sinless men.' See Barth 1968, p. 167.
3 'It's a sin', written by Neil Tennant/Chris Lowe. Published by Cage Music Ltd/Kobalt Music Publishing Ltd.
4 For a concise overview of sin in world religions, see https://www.newworldencyclopedia.org/entry/Sin
5 See Schulze Altcappenberg 2000, pp. 156–9, for Botticelli's drawing in context, and Traherne 2006 for an analysis of its theological meaning(s).
6 Dante 1995, p. 296.
7 For the idea of sin as a 'burden', see Anderson 2009, pp. 15–26.
8 For an analysis of Augustine's thought on pride, see Patout Burns 1988.
9 Dante 1995, p. 261.
10 See, for instance, Rubin 2007, pp. 144–6, who singles out the drawing for *Purgatorio X*.
11 For Brueghel's 'Paradise Landscapes' see Faber Kolb 2005, pp. 46–59; Ertz and Nitze-Ertz 2008–10, pp. 428–60; and Honig 2016, pp. 177–92.
12 See Greenblatt 2017 for Adam and Eve's cultural afterlife.
13 André Grabar notes that the motif of Adam and Eve was not popular in the art of the earliest Christians, and that this omission is perhaps the result of 'the deliberate intention of representing only the promise of salvation (and not anything that could be an obstacle to it)'. See Grabar 1968, pp. 12–13.
14 Augustine developed the concept of Original Sin in his *Contra Julianum* (Against Julian) and *De nuptiis et concupiscentia* (On Marriage and Concupiscence): Augustine 1957 and Augustine 1955. For an introduction to the concept and its genesis and influence, see Fredriksen 2012, pp. 93–134, and Greenblatt 2017, pp. 81–119.
15 Fredriksen 2012, p. 122.
16 London 2007, p. 65.
17 Bede 1969, p. 101.
18 See for instance Ozment 2011.
19 Miller 1970, p. 274.
20 Nickel 1982, p. 127, n. 21.
21 This theory is based on an entry in the register of Wittenberg University dated 5 October 1517, which mentions a certain 'Johannes Sonder de Wittenbergk', whom some scholars have identified as the painter's son Hans. See Kunz 1995, p. 126, n. 14.
22 Levi D'Ancona 1957, pp. 27–8.
23 For this concept, see McCue 1980.
24 Kauffmann 2003, p. 231.
25 For this iconographic tradition, see Bonnell 1917.
26 Battaglia et al. 2011, pp. 1–6. The other pictures were Michelangelo's *Creation of Adam* and a *Dead Christ with Angels* by Giovanni Bellini.
27 '*GE.3. MVLIERIS SEMEN HIS. SERPENTIS CAPUT CONTRIVIT*.' For the translation, see Ainsworth 2010, pp. 173–9.
28 For the development of this iconography, see Settis 1975 and Pierguidi 2009.
29 Colantuono 2006, p. 65.
30 Ibid., pp. 65, 68, n. 56.
31 For a comparison and analysis of Cranach's mythological subjects in the light of *Adam and Eve*, see S. Foister in London 2007, pp. 46–61. For Cranach's relationship with the female subject, see Ozment 2011, pp. 173–250.
32 Berger 1972, p. 51.
33 For a perceptive account on meaningful ambiguity in the depiction of Venus/Eve/Mary, see Rubin 2000. Steven Ozment sees all of what he call's 'Cranach's women' in a positive Protestant sexual light, whether they are Eve *or* Venus, see Ozment 2011, esp. p. 250.
34 See also Pérez d'Ors 2007, p. 97, and London 2007, pp. 80–1.
35 T.J. Clark analogously describes this as 'painting's muteness': Clark 2018, p. 10.
36 Los Angeles 2018, pp. 104–5.
37 For a stimulating comparison between Bronzino's *Allegory* ('bad love') and his *Deposition of Christ* ('good love') touching on similar themes, see Polhemus 1990, pp. 10–15.
38 Vasari 1979, p. 2073.
39 Erwin Panofsky's is one of the more influential readings: 'Luxury, surrounded by personifications of and symbols of treacherous pleasures and manifest evils; this group now is unveiled by Time and Truth.' See Panofsky 1939, p. 90. Paul Barolsky rightly notes that many interpretations have led to what the author calls 'some of the more amusing fictions of modern art-historical investigations', and that the picture was never meant to be precisely 'decoded'. See Barolsky 2006, p. 24. For a concise overview of the picture's vast bibliography, see Cox-Rearick 1995, p. 227.
40 See for instance Clark 1956, pp. 128–9, and Grantham Turner 2017, pp. 321–2.
41 Most notably Conway 1986 and Healy 1997.

42 Anderson 1994, p. 19.
43 Ibid., p. 20.
44 Ibid.
45 Rubin 2018, pp. 99, 238, n. 26.
46 Avery-Quash 2015, p. 852.
47 For the perhaps unexpected kinship between Courbet's *Burial at Ornans* (Musée d'Orsay, Paris) and Bronzino's *Deposition* (Musée des Beaux-Arts et d'Archéologie, Besançon), see Levine 1991.
48 For a good summary of this outrage, see A. Dumas in New York 1988, pp. 133–5.
49 Nochlin 1988, pp. 34–6.
50 Gregory the Great 1979–85. The English translation is Gregory the Great 1844–50.
51 For the different 'lists', see Bloomfield 1952, pp. 69–79. Bloomfield's is the authoritative study on the conception and history of the seven deadly sins. Two valuable edited volumes addressing the afterlife of the seven deadly sins are Newhauser 2007 and Newhauser and Ridyard 2012. For the visual tradition of the seven deadly sins (in the broadest sense), see Bern 2010.
52 *The Seven Deadly Sins* has an extensive bibliography, but the state of the scholarship is summarised in Ilsink et al. 2016, pp. 468–75.
53 See Koerner 2006 for a stimulating discussion on the *ira* section of the painting.
54 In his *Comentarios de la pintura*, the Spanish humanist Felipe de Guevara refers to the painting as *mesa* (table). Guevara uses '*mesa*' strictly referring to tables in this context (*mesa* could mean panel in different contexts). See Ilsink et al. 2016, pp. 468, 473–4.
55 Tait 1991, pp. 142–60.
56 Tait's view of animal symbolism and sin is interesting in regard to the paintings by Jan Brueghel the Elder and Lucas Cranach that show many animals (p. 151): '... the frequent portrayal of the Sins as animals in Western European medieval literature since the thirteenth century did not result in any consistent use of the symbolism in medieval and Renaissance art.'
57 For the origins of this expression, see Kloek 1998, pp. 7–13.
58 '*zyn schilderyen zyn als zyn levenswyze, en zyn levenswyze als zijn schilderyen*', see Kloek 1998, p. 7. For the complete biography, see Houbraken 1953, vol. III, pp. 10–20.
59 Benvenuto Cellini's sixteenth-century autobiography is a famous example. See Cellini 1949. The classic study on the 'character and conduct' of artists is Wittkower and Wittkower 1963. See for instance the section titled 'Debauchery among Sixteenth- and Seventeenth-Century Artists', pp. 159–61.
60 Washington DC 1996, p. 224.
61 MacLaren 1991, vol. 1, p. 431.
62 See Westermann 1997, pp. 111–12 for ideas about decorum in Steen's environment.
63 See for instance Antal 1962, pp. 95–6.
64 Gombrich 1995, p. 462.
65 Bindman 1970.
66 For a summary of Hogarth's story, the individual pictures, and related works and objects, see Riding 2006.
67 Ibid., p. 142.
68 Solkin 2000.
69 Apuleius 1996, p. 219.
70 Ibid., p. 221. Apuleius' story found its way to the painter via Jean de La Fontaine's *Les Amours de Psyché et de Cupidon*, first published in 1669. See Wine 2018, pp. 206–9.
71 Ibid., p. 205.
72 Campbell 2014, p. 658.
73 An exhibition dedicated to the theme of salvation through Christ was held in the National Gallery in 2000. See London 2000.
74 Steinmetz 1994.
75 Anderson 2009, pp. 8–9.
76 Taylor 1997, p. 88.
77 For this controversy and its interpreters, see ibid., pp. 4–5, 262–8.
78 Koerner 2004, pp. 177–8.
79 Buried below Raphael's altarpiece in his chapel in the church of San Domenico in Città di Castello, the picture's patron Domenico Gavari would have been second in line to receive the redemptive blood. For the altarpiece's original context, see Henry 2002, pp. 268–78.
80 For this picture, on long term loan to the National Gallery from the Society of Antiquaries, see J.A. Franklin's catalogue entry in Franklin et al. 2015, pp. 216–28.
81 Ibid., p. 224. The second woman reading a book has been associated with Mary Magdalene, Saint Bridget of Sweden and the lesser-known Abbess Humility of Faenza.
82 The panel touches on a number of arboreal theological themes, most obviously the Crucifixion, but also the Tree of Jesse (Christ's family tree going back to King David's father Jesse) and the Tree of Life from Genesis. See Franklin et al. 2015, p. 220.
83 Campbell 1998, p. 262.
84 John the Baptist carries a scroll with an inscription about sin

from the First Letter of Peter (1: 18–19): 'You know that you were ransomed from the futile ways inherited from your ancestors, not with perishable things like silver or gold, but with the precious blood of Christ, like that of a lamb without defect or blemish.'

85 Flaubert 1910.

86 El Greco seems to have based his painting on an 'enhanced' version of the scriptures, Angelico Buonriccio's *Le pie, et christiane parafrasi sopra l'Evangelio di San Matteo, et di San Giovanni*, a text with a strong emphasis on Christ's raging anger during this episode. See Casper 2014, pp. 96–105.

87 See Koerner 2004, pp. 289–303.

88 See for instance *A Million Little Pieces* author James Frey's impression of Warhol's *Repent*: '"I can imagine Warhol sitting there," he continued, of *Repent and Sin No More*, a 1985 silkscreen of just those words against a black canvas ... "and having a conversation with somebody, and talking about sex and drugs, and somebody says, 'Repent and sin no more'."' Quoted in R. Gardner, 'A Divine Intervention', *The Wall Street Journal*, 8 October 2010.

89 Milwaukee 2009, p. 33.

90 Richardson 1992, p. 140.

91 For examples, see London 2017, pp. 27–52, and Garnett and Rosser 2013, pp. 211–13.

92 De Voragine 1993, vol. I, p. 375.

93 In Veronese's case, the source is likely to have been Pietro Aretino's *La humanità di Christo* of 1535 instead of the *Golden Legend*, see Rosand 2011. Nicholas Penny identified the picture's possible subject as *Christ healing a Woman with an Issue of Blood* (?), see Penny 2008, pp. 334–43.

94 Rosand 2011, p. 393.

95 For a good summary of this debate in an artistic context, see Goffen 1986, pp. 73–106.

96 Cited in Hodne 2012, p. 49–50.

97 For the iconographic tradition in Spain, see Stratton 1994 (see pp. 70–87 for the Spanish debate on the doctrine). For the larger iconographic tradition, see Levi D'Ancona 1957 and Hodne 2012.

98 See Tiffany 2012, pp. 23–48 for the context of *The Immaculate Conception*.

99 Cited in Bronkhurst 2006, p. 180.

100 See ibid., pp. 177–8 for the Manchester picture and pp. 179–81 for the larger version in the Lady Lever Art Gallery.

101 For Hunt's travels and their meaning for *The Scapegoat*, see Boime 2002.

102 Bonhoeffer 1954, p. 89.

103 De Voragine 1993, vol. II, p. 148.

104 Campbell 2014, pp. 793–5.

105 For the lost altarpiece, see Hinkle 1965, pp. 111–13, and Campbell 2014, pp. 796–7.

106 Campbell 2014, p. 805, n. 73.

107 For an exploration of what 'confessional' could mean in Emin's oeuvre and biography, see Lake Smith 2017.

108 See Emin and Jones 2017, pp. 74–5, for a close-up and installation view of *For You*.

109 For more explicit examples, see ibid., pp. 104–5, 224.

110 Oliver 2004, pp. 19–39.

111 Ibid., p. 38.

112 Ibid., pp. 39–56.

113 *Christ and the Woman taken in Adultery* belongs to a small group of similar small-scale grisailles painted by Bruegel, see Grossmann 1952.

114 T.J. Clark rightly calls Bruegel 'the monarch of down-to-earthness': Clark 2018, p. 78.

115 The most sensitive 'exegesis' of this picture is Melion 2014.

116 For the engravings and their preparatory drawings, see Sellink 2007, pp. 92–109.

117 The first, a miniature on ivory painted in Rome, is lost. The two larger versions are in Rotterdam (Museum Boijmans Van Beuningen) and Vienna (Kunsthistorisches Museum). See Morra 2007.

118 See London 2003.

119 See for instance Rosen 2015, p. 212.

120 Dante 1995, p. 358. For an analysis of this passage, see Brownlee 1978.

# BIBLIOGRAPHY

All Bible passages (unless stated otherwise) come from the New Revised Standard Version, anglicised edition (NRSVA); see *The Holy Bible containing the Old and New Testaments with the Apocryphal/Deuterocanonical Books, New Revised Standard Version, anglicised edition*, Oxford 1995

AINSWORTH 2010
M.W. Ainsworth (ed.), *Man, Myth, and Sensual Pleasures: Jan Gossart's Renaissance: The Complete Works*, New Haven and London 2010

ANDERSON 2009
G.A. Anderson, *Sin: A History*, New Haven and London 2009

ANDERSON 1994
J. Anderson, 'A "most improper picture": Transformations of Bronzino's Erotic Allegory', *Apollo*, vol. 139 (February 1994), pp. 19–28

ANTAL 1962
F. Antal, *Hogarth and his Place in European Art*, London 1962

APULEIUS 1996
Apuleius, *Metamorphoses (The Golden Ass), Volume I: Books 1–6*, ed. and trans. J.A. Hanson, Cambridge, MA 1996

AUGUSTINE 1955
Augustine, 'On Marriage and Concupiscence', in *St. Augustine: Anti-Pelagian Writings, Vol. 5*, ed. P. Schaff, Grand Rapids, MI 1955, pp. 457–532

AUGUSTINE 1957
Augustine, *Saint Augustine Against Julian*, trans. M.A. Schumacher, New York 1957

AVERY-QUASH 2015
S. Avery-Quash, 'The Art of Conservation II: Sir Charles Eastlake and Conservation at the National Gallery, London', *The Burlington Magazine*, vol. 157, no. 1353 (2015), pp. 846–54

BAROLSKY 2006
P. Barolsky, 'Bronzino Fictions', *Source: Notes in the History of Art*, vol. 25, no. 2 (2006), pp. 23–5

BARTH 1968
K. Barth, *The Epistle to the Romans*, Oxford 1968

BATTAGLIA ET AL. 2011
F. Battaglia, S.H. Lisanby and D. Freedberg, 'Corticomotor Excitability during Observation and Imagination of a Work of Art', *Frontiers in Human Neuroscience*, vol. 5 (2011), pp. 1–6

BEDE 1969
Bede, *Bede's Ecclesiastical History of the English People*, ed. B. Colgrave and R.A.B. Mynors, Oxford 1969

BERGER 1972
J. Berger, *Ways of Seeing*, London 1972

BERN 2010
B. Müller et al., *Lust und Laster: Die 7 Todsünden von Dürer bis Nauman*, exh. cat., Kunstmuseum Bern and Zentrum Paul Klee, Bern 2010

BINDMAN 1970
D. Bindman, 'Hogarth's "Satan, Sin and Death" and its Influence', *The Burlington Magazine*, vol. 112, no. 804 (1970), pp. 153–9

BLOOMFIELD 1952
M.W. Bloomfield, *The Seven Deadly Sins: An Introduction to the History of a Religious Concept, with Special Reference to Medieval English Literature*, East Lansing, MI 1952

BOIME 2002
A. Boime, 'William Holman Hunt's "The Scapegoat": Rite of Forgiveness/Transference of Blame', *The Art Bulletin*, vol. 84, no. 1 (2002), pp. 94–114

BONHOEFFER 1954
D. Bonhoeffer, *Life Together*, trans. J.W. Doberstein, London 1954

BONNELL 1917
J.K. Bonnell, 'The Serpent with a Human Head in Art and in Mystery Play', *American Journal of Archaeology*, vol. 21, no. 3 (1917), pp. 255–91

BRONKHURST 2006
J. Bronkhurst, *William Holman Hunt: A Catalogue Raisonné*, 2 vols, New Haven and London 2006

BROWNLEE 1978
K. Brownlee, 'Dante and Narcissus (Purg. XXX, 76–99)', *Dante Studies, with the Annual Report of the Dante Society*, vol. 96 (1978), pp. 201–6

CAMPBELL 1998
L. Campbell, *National Gallery Catalogues: The Fifteenth Century Netherlandish Schools*, London 1998

CAMPBELL 2014
L. Campbell, *National Gallery Catalogues: The Sixteenth Century Netherlandish Paintings with French Paintings before 1600*, London 2014

CASPER 2014
A.R. Casper, *Art and the Religious Image in El Greco's Italy*, University Park, PA 2014

CELLINI 1949
B. Cellini, *The Life of Benvenuto Cellini, Written by Himself*, trans. J.A. Symonds, London 1949

CLARK 1956
K. Clark, *The Nude: A Study of Ideal Art*, London 1956

CLARK 2018
T.J. Clark, *Heaven on Earth: Painting and the Life to Come*, London 2018

COLANTUONO 2006
A. Colantuono, 'Caravaggio's Literary Culture', in *Caravaggio: Realism, Rebellion, Reception*, ed. G. Warwick, Newark, DE 2006, pp. 57–68

CONWAY 1986
J.F. Conway, 'Syphilis and Bronzino's London Allegory', *Journal of the Warburg and Courtauld Institutes*, vol. 49 (1986), pp. 250–5

COX-REARICK 1995
J. Cox-Rearick, *The Collection of Francis I: Royal Treasures*, Antwerp and New York 1995

DANTE 1995
Dante Alighieri, *The Divine Comedy*, trans. A. Mandelbaum, New York 1995

DE VORAGINE 1993
J. de Voragine, *The Golden Legend: Readings on the Saints*, 2 vols, trans. W.G. Ryan, Princeton 1993

EMIN AND JONES 2017
T. Emin and J. Jones, *Tracey Emin, Works 2007–2017*, New York 2017

ERTZ AND NITZE-ERTZ 2008–10
K. Ertz and C. Nitze-Ertz, *Jan Brueghel der Ältere (1568–1625): Kritischer Katalog der Gemälde, Band II, Landschaften mit christlichen Themen; Mythologie*, Lingen 2008–10

FABER KOLB 2005
A. Faber Kolb, *Jan Brueghel the Elder: The Entry of the Animals into Noah's Ark*, Los Angeles 2005

FLAUBERT 1910
G. Flaubert, *The Temptation of Saint Anthony*, trans. G.F. Monkshood, London 1910

FRANKLIN ET AL. 2015
J.A. Franklin, B. Nurse and P. Tudor-Craig, *Catalogue of Paintings in the Collection of the Society of Antiquaries of London*, Turnhout 2015

FREDRIKSEN 2012
P. Fredriksen, *Sin: The Early History of an Idea*, Princeton and Oxford 2012

GARNETT AND ROSSER 2013
J. Garnett and G. Rosser, *Spectacular Miracles: Transforming Images in Italy from the Renaissance to the Present*, London 2013

GOFFEN 1986
R. Goffen, *Piety and Patronage in Renaissance Venice: Bellini, Titian, and the Franciscans*, New Haven and London 1986

GOMBRICH 1995
E.H. Gombrich, *The Story of Art* (16th edn), London 1995

GRABAR 1968
A. Grabar, *Christian Iconography: A Study of its Origins*, Princeton 1968

GRANTHAM TURNER 2017
J. Grantham Turner, *Eros Visible: Art, Sexuality and Antiquity in Renaissance Italy*, New Haven and London 2017

GREENBLATT 2017
S. Greenblatt, *The Rise and Fall of Adam and Eve*, London 2017

GREGORY THE GREAT 1844–50
Gregory the Great, *Morals on the Book of Job*, 3 vols, Oxford 1844–50

GREGORY THE GREAT 1979–85
Gregory the Great, *Moralia in Job*, ed. M. Adriaen, 3 vols, Turnhout 1979–85

GROSSMANN 1952
F. Grossmann 'Bruegel's "Woman Taken in Adultery" and Other Grisailles', *The Burlington Magazine*, vol. 94, no. 593 (1952), pp. 218–29

HEALY 1997
M. Healy, 'Bronzino's London "Allegory" and the Art of Syphilis', *Oxford Art Journal*, vol. 20, no. 1 (1997), pp. 3–11

HENRY 2002
T. Henry, 'Raphael's Altar-Piece Patrons in Citta di Castello', *The Burlington Magazine*, vol. 144, no. 1190 (2002), pp. 268–78

HINKLE 1965
W.M. Hinkle, 'The Iconography of the Four Panels by the Master of Saint Giles', *Journal of the Warburg and Courtauld Institutes*, vol. 28 (1965), pp. 111–44

HODNE 2012
L. Hodne, *The Virginity of the Virgin: A Study in Marian Iconography*, Rome 2012

HONIG 2016
E.A. Honig, *Jan Brueghel and the Senses of Scale*, University Park, PA, 2016

HOUBRAKEN 1953
A. Houbraken, *De Groote Schouburgh der Nederlantsche Konstschilders en Schilderessen*, ed. P.T.A. Swillens, 3 vols, Maastricht 1943–53

ILSINK ET AL. 2016
M. Ilsink et al., *Hieronymus Bosch: Painter and Draughtsman, Catalogue Raisonné*, Brussels 2016

KAUFFMANN 2003
C.M. Kauffmann, *Biblical Imagery in Medieval England, 700–1550*, London and Turnhout 2003

KLOEK 1998
W.T. Kloek, *Een Huishouden van Jan Steen*, Hilversum 1998

KOERNER 2004
J.L. Koerner, *The Reformation of the Image*, London 2004

KOERNER 2006
J.L. Koerner, 'Bosch's Enmity', in *Tributes in Honor of James Marrow: Studies in Painting and Manuscript Illumination of the Late Middle Ages and Northern Renaissance*, ed. J.F. Hamburger and A.S. Korteweg, Turnhout 2006, pp. 285–300

KUNZ 1995
A. Kunz, 'Cranach as Cartographer: The Rediscovered "Map of the Holy Land"', *Print Quarterly*, vol. 12, no. 2 (1995), pp. 123–44

LAKE SMITH 2017
L. Lake Smith, 'Telling Stories: Performing Authenticity in the Confessional Art of Tracey Emin', *Rethinking History*, vol. 21, no. 2 (2017), pp. 296–309

LEVI D'ANCONA 1957
M. Levi D'Ancona, *The Iconography of the Immaculate Conception in the Middle Ages and Early Renaissance*, New York 1957

LEVINE 1991
S.Z. Levine, 'Courbet, Bronzino, and Blasphemy', *New Literary History*, vol. 22, no. 3 (1991), pp. 677–714

LONDON 2000
G. Finaldi et al., *The Image of Christ*, exh. cat., National Gallery, London 2000

LONDON 2003
S. Greeves and C. Wiggins, *Ron Mueck*, exh. cat., National Gallery, London 2003

LONDON 2007
C. Campbell (ed.), *Temptation in Eden: Lucas Cranach's 'Adam and Eve'*, exh. cat., Courtauld Gallery, London 2007

LONDON 2017
J. Sliwka, 'Painting the Sacred', in *Monochrome: Painting in Black and White*, L. Packer and J. Sliwka, exh. cat., National Gallery, London 2017, pp. 27–49

LOS ANGELES 2018
T. Kren (ed.), *The Renaissance Nude*, exh. cat., J. Paul Getty Museum, Los Angeles 2018

MACLAREN 1991
N. MacLaren, *National Gallery Catalogues: The Dutch School 1600–1900* (revised and expanded by C. Brown), 2 vols, London 1991

MCCUE 1980
J.F. McCue, '"Simul iustus et peccator" in Augustine, Aquinas, and Luther: Toward Putting the Debate in Context', *Journal of the American Academy of Religion*, vol. 48, no. 1 (1980), pp. 81–96

MELION 2014
W.S. Melion, 'Introduction: Visual Exegesis and Pieter Bruegel's "Christ and the Woman Taken in Adultery"', in *Imago Exegetica: Visual Images as Exegetical Instruments, 1400–1700*, ed. W.S. Melion, J. Clifton and M. Weemans, Leiden and Boston 2014, pp. 1–41

MILLER 1970
A.A. Miller, 'The Theologies of Luther and Boehme in the Light of their Genesis Commentaries', *The Harvard Theological Review*, vol. 63, no. 2 (1970), pp. 261–303

MILWAUKEE 2009
J.D. Ketner II, 'Warhol's Last Decade: Reinventing Painting', in *Andy Warhol: The Last Decade*, ed. J.D. Ketner II, exh. cat., Milwaukee Art Museum et al., 2009, pp. 14–47

MORRA 2007
J. Morra, 'Utopia Lost: Allegory, Ruins and Pieter Bruegel's Tower of Babel', *Art History*, vol. 30, no. 2 (2007), pp. 198–216

NEWHAUSER 2007
R.G. Newhauser (ed.), *The Seven Deadly Sins: From Communities to Individuals*, Leiden and Boston 2007

NEWHAUSER AND RIDYARD 2012
R.G. Newhauser and S.J. Ridyard (eds), *Sin in Medieval and Early Modern Culture: The Tradition of the Seven Deadly Sins*, York 2012

NEW YORK 1988
S. Faunce and L. Nochlin (eds), *Courbet Reconsidered*, exh. cat., Brooklyn Museum, New York 1988

NICKEL 1982
H. Nickel, '"The Judgement of Paris" by Lucas Cranach the Elder: Nature, Allegory, and Alchemy', *Metropolitan Museum Journal*, vol. 16 (1982), pp. 117–29

NOCHLIN 1988
L. Nochlin, 'Courbet's Real Allegory: Rereading the "Painter's Studio", Part Two: Ending with the Beginning: The Centrality of Gender', in New York 1988, pp. 16–41

OLIVER 2004
L. Oliver, *Boris Anrep: The National Gallery Mosaics*, London 2004

OZMENT 2011
S. Ozment, *The Serpent and the Lamb: Cranach, Luther, and the Making of the Reformation*, New Haven and London 2011

PANOFSKY 1939
E. Panofsky, *Studies in Iconology: Humanistic Themes in the Art of the Renaissance*, New York and Oxford 1939

PATOUT BURNS 1988
J. Patout Burns, 'Augustine on the Origin and Progress of Evil', *The Journal of Religious Ethics*, vol. 16, no. 1 (1988), pp. 9–27

PENNY 2008
N. Penny, *National Gallery Catalogues: The Sixteenth Century Italian Paintings, Vol. II: Venice 1540–1600*, London 2008

PÉREZ D'ORS 2007
P. Pérez d'Ors, 'A Lutheran Idyll: Lucas Cranach the Elder's "Cupid Complaining to Venus"', *Renaissance Studies*, vol. 21, no. 1 (2007), pp. 85–98

PIERGUIDI 2009
S. Pierguidi, 'Nascita e diffusione di una rara iconografia dell'Immacolata Concezione: da Figino e Caravaggio a Bourdon e Quellinus II', *Arte Lombarda*, vol. 157, no. 3 (2009), pp. 39–48

POLHEMUS 1990
R.M. Polhemus, *Erotic Love: Being in Love from Jane Austen to D.H. Lawrence*, Chicago and London 1990

RICHARDSON 1992
J. Richardson, 'Eulogy for Andy Warhol', in *Andy Warhol: Heaven and Hell Are Just One Breath Away! Late Paintings and Related Works, 1984–1986*, New York 1992, pp. 140–1

RIDING 2006
C. Riding, 'Marriage A-la-Mode', in *Hogarth*, ed. M. Hallett and C. Riding, London 2006, pp. 140–57

ROSAND 2011
D. Rosand, 'Veronese's Magdalene and Pietro Aretino', *The Burlington Magazine*, vol. 153, no. 1299 (2011), pp. 392–4

ROSEN 2015
A. Rosen, *Art + Religion in the 21st Century*, London 2015

RUBIN 2000
P. Rubin, 'The Seductions of Antiquity', in *Manifestations of Venus: Art and Sexuality*, ed. C. Arscott and K. Scott, Manchester 2000, pp. 24–38

RUBIN 2007
P. Rubin, *Images and Identity in Fifteenth-Century Florence*, New Haven and London 2007

RUBIN 2018
P. Rubin, *Seen from Behind: Perspectives on the Male Body and Renaissance Art*, New Haven and London 2018

SCHULZE ALTCAPPENBERG 2000
H.T. Schulze Altcappenberg, *Sandro Botticelli: Der Bilderzyklus zu Dantes Göttlicher Komödie*, Ostfildern-Ruit 2000

SELLINK 2007
M. Sellink, *Bruegel: The Complete Paintings, Drawings and Prints*, Brussels 2007

SETTIS 1975
S. Settis, 'Immagini della meditazione, dell'incertezza e del pentimento nell'arte antica', *Prospettiva*, no. 2 (1975), pp. 4–18

SOLKIN 2000
D.H. Solkin, 'The Fetish over the Fireplace: Disease as "genius loci" in Hogarth's "Marriage A-la-Mode"', *The British Art Journal*, vol. 2, no. 1 (2000), pp. 26–34

STEINMETZ 1994
D. Steinmetz, 'Vineyard, Farm, and Garden: The Drunkenness of Noah in the Context of Primeval History', *Journal of Biblical Literature*, vol. 113, no. 2 (1994), pp. 193–207

STRATTON 1994
S.L. Stratton, *The Immaculate Conception in Spanish Art*, Cambridge 1994

TAIT 1991
H. Tait, *Catalogue of the Waddesdon Bequest in the British Museum, Vol. III: The 'Curiosities'*, London 1991

TAYLOR 1997
J. Taylor, *John the Baptist within Second Temple Judaism*, London 1997

TIFFANY 2012
T.J. Tiffany, *Diego Velázquez's Early Paintings and the Culture of Seventeenth-Century Seville*, University Park, PA 2012

TRAHERNE 2006
M. Traherne, 'Ekphrasis and Eucharist: The Poetics of Seeing God's Art in *Purgatorio X*', *The Italianist*, vol. 26, no. 2 (2006), pp. 177–96

TWAIN 1894
M. Twain, *The Tragedy of Pudd'nhead Wilson and the Comedy of those Extraordinary Twins*, Hartford, CT 1894

VASARI 1979
G. Vasari, *Lives of the Most Eminent Painters Sculptors and Architects*, trans. G. Du C. de Vere, New York 1979

WASHINGTON DC 1996
H. Perry Chapman, W.T. Kloek and A.K. Wheelock Jr., *Jan Steen: Painter and Storyteller*, exh. cat., National Gallery of Art, Washington DC 1996

WESTERMANN 1997
M. Westermann, *The Amusements of Jan Steen*, Zwolle 1997

WINE 2018
H. Wine, *National Gallery Catalogues: The Eighteenth Century French Paintings*, London 2018

WITTKOWER AND WITTKOWER 1963
R. Wittkower and M. Wittkower, *Born Under Saturn: The Character and Conduct of Artists: A Documented History from Antiquity to the French Revolution*, London 1963

# LIST OF EXHIBITED WORKS

Master of Saint Giles
(active about 1500)
*The Mass of Saint Giles*, about 1500
Oil on oak, 62.3 × 46 cm
The National Gallery, London
Presented by the Art Fund, 1933
NG4681, **62**

Lucas Cranach the Elder
(1472–1553)
*Adam and Eve*, 1526
Oil on wood, 117.1 × 80.8 cm
On loan from The Samuel
Courtauld Trust,
The Courtauld Gallery, London
P.1947.LF.77, **5**

Jan Gossaert (Jean Gossart)
(active 1508; died 1532)
*The Virgin and Child*, 1527
Oil on oak, 30.7 × 24.3 cm
The National Gallery, London
NG1888, **9**

Lucas Cranach the Elder
(1472–1553)
*Venus and Cupid*, 1529
Oil on wood, 38.1 × 23.5 cm
The National Gallery, London
A gift from the Drue Heinz
Charitable Trust, 2018
NG6680, **11**

Bronzino (1503–1572)
*An Allegory with Venus
and Cupid*, about 1545
Oil on wood, 146.1 × 116.2 cm
The National Gallery, London
NG651, **16**

Pieter Bruegel the Elder
(active from 1550/1; died 1569)
*Christ and the Woman taken
in Adultery*, 1565
Oil on wood, 24.1 × 34.4 cm
On loan from The Samuel
Courtauld Trust,
The Courtauld Gallery, London
P.1978.PG.48, **70**

Jan Brueghel the Elder (1568–1625)
*The Garden of Eden*, 1613
Oil on copper, 23.7 × 36.8 cm
On loan from private collection,
Hong Kong
**2**

Diego Velázquez
(1599–1660)
*The Immaculate
Conception*, 1618–19
Oil on canvas, 135 × 101.6 cm
The National Gallery, London
Bought with the aid
of the Art Fund, 1974
NG6424, **56**

Jan Steen (1626–1679)
*The Effects of Intemperance*,
about 1663–5
Oil on wood, 76 × 106.5 cm
The National Gallery, London
NG6442, **24**

William Hogarth (1697–1764)
*Marriage A-la-Mode:
2, The Tête à Tête*, about 1743
Oil on canvas, 69.9 × 90.8 cm
The National Gallery, London
NG114, **28**

William Holman Hunt (1827–1910)
*The Scapegoat*, 1854–5
Oil on canvas, 33.7 × 45.9 cm
Manchester Art Gallery
1906.2, **58**

Andy Warhol (1928–1987)
*Repent, and Sin No More!
(Positive and Negative)*, 1985–6
Acrylic paint and silkscreen
on canvas, each 50.8 × 40.6 cm
Ed Freedman, Los Angeles,
CA, USA
**52**

Ron Mueck (born 1958)
*Youth*, 2009
Mixed media, 65 × 28 × 16 cm
Courtesy the artist
**73**

Tracey Emin (born 1963)
*It was just a kiss*, 2010
Neon lights, 57.7 × 97.3 cm
Exhibition Copy, Courtesy
of the Artist and White Cube.
Original 2010 version
illustrated on p. 82, **62**

# LENDERS

Hong Kong
Private collection

London
The Courtauld Gallery
The National Gallery
Tracey Emin/White Cube
Ron Mueck

Los Angeles
Ed Freedman

Manchester
Manchester Art Gallery

# ACKNOWLEDGEMENTS

Joost Joustra

The publication of this book and the exhibition it accompanies would not have been possible without the generous support of Howard and Roberta Ahmanson. To them, I would like to express my deepest gratitude. The generosity of the lenders to *Sin* has known no bounds, and I am very grateful to them all.

Without Susanna Avery-Quash's unfailing support and care this project would not have been possible. It has been an absolute pleasure working with her every step of the way. Gabriele Finaldi, Susan Foister, Caroline Campbell, Jane Knowles and Christine Riding have supported *Sin* from the outset, and Christine's and Susanna's guidance has been fundamental throughout every phase. All my colleagues in the Curatorial Department have generously shared their knowledge and experience, but I would like to single out Bart Cornelis, Rebecca Gill, Daniel Herrmann, Letizia Treves, Francesca Whitlum-Cooper and Matthias Wivel. Many chats and cups of coffee with my 'fellow fellows' were of vital importance. At the National Gallery, I would also like to thank Christina Bradstreet, Alan Brooks, Andrew Bruce, Alice Calloway, Belén Cao, Harriet Davison, Gracie Divall, Neil Evans, Anne Fay, Julie Firth, Jonathan Franklin, Joseph Kendra, Elizabeth Loughran, Alexandra Moskalenko, Anna Murray, Britta New, Chris Oberon, Belinda Phillpot, Margaux Portron, Tess Raven, Eleanor Richards and Janet Skeet. Katherine Miller's expert guidance and patience have been crucial, and working with her has been a delight.

The National Gallery Company have made writing this book a joyous experience. I would in particular like to thank Jan Green, Suzanne Bosman, Jane Hyne and Amanda Mackie. My editor, Elin Sandell, is as much responsible for this book as I am, and I could not have done it without her. I am also grateful to Kate Bell and Rachel Giles for their work on the text, and to Kathrin Jacobsen for designing the book.

Beyond the Gallery, I am grateful for the wisdom of Alixe Bovey, Charles Clarke, Iona Keen, Ayla Lepine, Vittorio Montemaggi, Scott Nethersole, Jennifer Sliwka and my students on the Christianity & the Arts MA course at King's College, London. Ben Quash's erudition and eloquence have been indispensable. As always, Olivia has been both my rock and my fiercest editor.

# PHOTOGRAPHIC CREDITS

All images © The National Gallery, London, unless credited otherwise.

BERLIN Kupferstichkabinett, Staatliche Museen, Berlin © Photo Scala, Florence/BPK, Bildagentur für Kunst, Kultur und Geschichte, Berlin: 1.

BIRMINGHAM Barber Institute of Fine Arts © The Trustees of the Barber Institute of Fine Arts, University of Birmingham: 14.

LIVERPOOL Liverpool Cathedral © Tracey Emin. All rights reserved, DACS/Artimage 2019. Image courtesy White Cube. Photo: Barry Hale: 64

LONDON The British Library, London © By Permission of The British Library, London / Bridgeman Images: 8.
The British Museum, London © The Trustees of The British Museum: 20, 21.
Courtauld Institute Gallery © The Samuel Courtauld Trust, The Courtauld Gallery, London: 5, 6, 13, 70. The National Gallery, London © The National Gallery, London / The Estate of Boris Anrep: 66, 67, 68, 69.
Royal Collection Trust / © Her Majesty Queen Elizabeth II 2020: 15.
Society of Antiquaries of London © Photo courtesy of the owner: 46.

MADRID Museo Nacional del Prado © Photographic Archive Museo Nacional del Prado: 22, 72.

MANCHESTER Manchester Art Gallery © Manchester Art Gallery / Bridgeman Images: 58, 59.

NEW YORK The Museum of Modern Art, New York 2019 © Bruce Nauman / Artists Rights Society (ARS), New York and DACS, London 2020. / Digital image, The Museum of Modern Art, New York/ Scala, Florence: 23.

PRIVATE COLLECTIONS
Courtesy the artist © Ron Mueck/ photo The National Gallery, London: 73.
Ed Freedman, Los Angeles, CA, USA © 2020 The Andy Warhol Foundation for the Visual Arts, Inc. / Licensed by DACS, London: 52.
Private collection, Hong Kong © Photo courtesy of the owner: 2.
Private collection © Tracey Emin. All rights reserved, DACS/Artimage 2020. Image courtesy the artist: 63.
Private collection © 2020 The Andy Warhol Foundation for the Visual Arts, Inc. / Licensed by DACS/ Artimage, London: 53, 54.

ROME Galleria Borghese © Galleria Borghese, Rome / Bridgeman Images: 10.

Published to accompany the exhibition

**SIN**

The National Gallery, London
15 April – 5 July 2020

Exhibition supported by
Howard and Roberta Ahmanson



This exhibition has been made possible by the provision of insurance through the Government Indemnity Scheme. The National Gallery would like to thank HM Government for providing Government Indemnity and the Department for Digital, Culture, Media and Sport and Arts Council England for arranging the indemnity.

First published in 2020 by
National Gallery Company Limited
St Vincent House
30 Orange Street
London WC2H 7HH
www.nationalgallery.co.uk

ISBN 978 1 85709 665 1
1049747

British Library Cataloguing-in-Publication Data
A catalogue record is available from the British Library

Library of Congress Control Number: 2019953614

All measurements give height before width

Publisher: Jan Green
Project Editor: Elin Sandell
Editor: Kate Bell
Designer: Kathrin Jacobsen
Picture Researcher: Suzanne Bosman
Production: Jane Hyne and Amanda Mackie

Printed in Belgium by Graphius
Colour origination by DL Imaging, London

Cover: Lucas Cranach the Elder, *Adam and Eve* (detail, **5**)
Pages 2–3: Jan Brueghel the Elder, *The Garden of Eden* (detail, **2**)
Page 4: Bronzino, *An Allegory with Venus and Cupid* (detail, **16**)
Page 7: Diego Velázquez, *The Immaculate Conception* (detail, **56**)
Page 8: Master of Saint Giles, *The Mass of Saint Giles* (detail, **62**)
Page 94: William Hogarth, *Marriage A-la-Mode: 2, The Tête à Tête* (detail, **28**)